FEAR
WAS NEVER AN OPTION

Bob Cary

FEAR

WAS NEVER
AN OPTION

Bob Cary

EAGLE EDITIONS
2006

EAGLE EDITIONS
AN IMPRINT OF HERITAGE BOOKS, INC.

Books, CDs, and more—Worldwide

For our listing of thousands of titles see our website
at
www.HeritageBooks.com

Cover art and interior illustrations
Copyright © 2005 Bob Cary

Published 2006 by
HERITAGE BOOKS, INC.
Publishing Division
65 East Main Street
Westminster, Maryland 21157-5026

Copyright © 2005 Bob Cary

International Standard Book Number: 0-7884-3227-3

Foreword

In every culture, there is a warrior clan. It consists of men and women, who by their genes, background, upbringing, or a combination thereof, do not hesitate to fight when their family, neighbors or nation is threatened. Some are professionals, skilled members of the armed forces. Many more are ordinary citizens who answer the call when a threat is present. In civilian life, we do not always know who the warriors are, but they exist among us. It is only when the forces of evil are unleashed that we discover their identity. They do not hesitate. They act. It has been true since the citizen riflemen at Lexington and Concord faced off against British regulars. It was apparent on September 11, 2001, when a handful of passengers on board Flight 93 determined that the hijackers would never reach their target. Most of the passengers on that flight were terrified, but not the handful. They knew what had to be done; they did it.

1

In times of peace, the warrior clan is not held in particular esteem. Indeed, in some instances, they are derided as unnecessary and uncivilized. It is only when a culture is threatened with extinction that they are appreciated.

Without question, war is brutal. It is one of the most heinous activities of the human race. There are those who say all matters can be settled by discussion, by negotiation, by peaceful means. True, there are times when this may work. But in my generation, we had the spectacle, over a number of years, of the Jews in Europe faced with the Nazi program of extermination. Jewish leaders urged restraint, negotiation, discussion, compliance. It did not save three million of them from death. There were peace debates and peace gatherings in 1941 aimed at keeping the U.S. out of World War II. Our diplomats were discussing peace with Japanese officials when we were attacked by the Japanese Navy at Pearl Harbor. For those who immediately volunteered for the Army, Air Force, Navy, Coast Guard or Marine Corps, we went because our nation, our neighbors and our families were threatened. For that we willingly laid our lives on the line.

The Marine Corps, in 1942, was made up of deer hunters from the North, elk hunters from the West, squirrel hunters from the South, duck hunters from the Midwest and grouse hunters from the East. Nearly every one of us knew how to shoot before we enlisted. In the Corps, we were well-trained, well-armed, expertly-led, highly-motivated and deadly. We were very good at what we did. Given the same circumstances we would readily do it again.

In most war books it is fashionable to include a considerable amount of profanity. Swearing is common among combat troops, but has little meaning; thus it is not a feature of this writing. This book mainly concerns one battalion of the Second Marine Division and what we did. It was over sixty years ago and some names have been substituted for names I can no longer recall. By military law, we were not allowed to carry a diary.

However, all the incidents described occurred as near as can be determined. The Marine Corps Museum in Washington, D.C. was very helpful with many details. So was former Staff Sergeant James Von Gremp of Camdenton, Missouri, my first squad leader, a professional who helped me get through the early fighting and was an example of dedication and courage.

Whenever I hear a band strike up a march, I can once again see the faces of the men I knew, the steely glint in their eyes as they hit the beaches, charging into the teeth of hell. I remember those who were blown to bloody pieces, those who went down torn by bullets or shell fragments and those of us who through the Grace of God came through relatively intact. We were warriors. We conducted ourselves as warriors without apology. Among these Marines, fear was never an option.

Dedication

This book is dedicated to our comrades in uniform who never made it home. Some are buried beneath green sod or raked coral in distant lands. Some were shipped home in caskets for reburial and lie in hometown cemeteries. Some died from their wounds on board ship and received a burial at sea. Some were hit with shells, bombs or mines and were blown to bits or so torn that they could not be identified. These became "soldiers known only to God." And so they remain.

Rest in peace, comrades. All of you served with courage and honor. Many of you gave your lives that the rest of us might live. All of you gave your lives that this nation might live in freedom. We salute you.

Chapter 1
The Day Our War Started

The island of Guadalcanal was a bright green horizontal strip separating the pale blue sky from a dark blue Pacific Ocean. As we went over the steel rail on the transport ship and climbed down rope cargo nets into waiting Higgins Boats, we didn't know what to expect. We were aware that the initial assault had been made on August 7 by elements of the First and Second Division. We also knew that some of the Second had stormed ashore first at Florida Island followed by landings on Tulalgi, Gavutu, Tanambogo and finally Guadalcanal. The first offensive of the war on Japanese-held territory had begun. And we also knew that other than a strong beachhead and occupation of the airfield on the northern coast, not much of Guadalcanal had been taken. This was now five months later, but we were sure there was still a lot of war going on. As our Higgins boats chugged toward the beach, platoon leaders warned: "Keep your heads down. When the boat hits the beach and the ramp goes down, get out quick, run for cover and don't bunch up!"

We knew the drill. When the hulls ground into the sand and the ramp dropped, we exited on a dead run and sprinted zig-zag toward the green line of coconut palm foliage marking the jungle rim. At the edge of the coconut trees, we slowed to a walk and then stopped. A half dozen Marines in their white under shorts were busy scrubbing clothes on a long wooden table in the shade. They stared at us in disbelief and we stared back.

"Where's the war?" somebody asked.

One of the scrubbers paused and jerked a thumb over his shoulder: "Two miles that way."

For a few seconds we stood there with our huge overseas packs and rifles, our steel helmets with the chinstraps buckled, feeling utterly ridiculous. That beach had been stormed five months earlier. The nearest live Japs were two miles distant. Command didn't pass the word down that we would be landing on a safe beach. Or maybe they thought it would be a good practice exercise for us to go ashore on a beach where no enemy was present, like the beaches we practiced on in California. Or maybe it was just a joke on us. We never did find out. It was one of those instances of total stupidity that occurs in a war and for which there are no answers.

Our officers recovered quickly, began yelling orders, formed us into columns and we marched into the coconut groves to look for whatever bivouac area the division might have assigned us. Our jeeps, trucks and heavy equipment came in behind us. For a couple of days we camped under the coconut trees, our main hazards being a few rounds of Jap artillery and Washing Machine Charley - one of several Japanese bombers that came over each night to lay sticks of bombs on the airfield. The tropical heat was ever-present and whole squadrons of mosquitoes regularly swarmed up from the rain-soaked mud to chew on us unceasingly. At night, legions of huge but harmless land crabs came out from beneath their hideouts and scuttled around on dead palm

8

leaves, making an unnerving clatter. Then orders came to load up and head for the front.

It had rained at daybreak, an everyday occurrence. The sun eventually came out, raising steam. Our convoy of trucks and jeeps lurched west up the muddy coastal road toward the Kokumbona River, where reports indicated a sticky fight was in progress. Sporadically, we heard the distant whump of artillery and mortar fire. Coconut groves pressing in on both sides of the winding road made for limited visibility ahead. Behind our particular 3/4 ton truck was a jeep pulling a 75mm pack howitzer. Ahead was another jeep with a gun in tow and in front of that we could make out the rear of another 3/4 ton truck. An explosion just ahead brought the convoy to a halt. A column of white smoke rose straight up.

"Land mine!" the word came back. "Hogan got hit." I jumped off the truck and ran forward to see if help was needed.

Corporal Hogan had been riding on the truck tailgate, rifle on his lap, legs dangling over. The right rear wheel of the truck had run over a Jap land mine which blew off the wheel and blew Hogan up in the air. The blast had ripped his legs, his chest and tore up his face. We lifted him gently to the side of the road and propped him up against the trunk of a coconut tree. Fox Battery corpsman, Tony Massaro came running, jerked open his first aid kit and tried to staunch the flow of blood. Hogan was a mess with his eyes gone and face shredded, but he was breathing and still conscious.

"How's it look?" Hogan managed to whisper. Tony shot him with morphine and shook his head in despair, tears starting to run down his cheeks. It was Tony's first casualty and it hit him hard.

Hogan's torn lips moved a little. "Gimme a cigarette."

Somebody lit up a cigarette and Tony stuck it in Hogan's mouth He took two big drags, shuddered and stopped breathing. The cigarette rolled down his chest, hissed in his blood and fell to the ground. First casualty. First death. Our eyes smarted with fury. We hadn't even gotten into the war and one man was dead. Grimly we climbed back on the trucks. The column moved ahead, avoiding the stalled truck and the dead body. The boom of artillery and mortar fire grew louder.

Hogan and I had gone through boot camp together at San Diego. He was a crack shot with a rifle and scored among the top four or five each day on the range. The first morning we were firing Colt .45's on the Camp Pendleton pistol range, Hogan set up a grumbling storm of profanity. The Range Officer walked over and inquired as to the trouble.

"This is a lousy way to shoot a handgun," Hogan complained. "How the hell can you hit anything with your left hand in your hip pocket, the pistol in your right hand waving around toward the target?'"

"How do you think it ought to be done?" the Range Officer inquired sarcastically.

Hogan squared off toward the target in a half crouch with both hands on the .45, waist high, in front.

"Whatta you some kind of a cowboy?" the Range Officer snarled. "Yeah," said Hogan, evenly.

"Hold your fire!" the Range Officer bellowed down the firing line. "The cowboy here is going to give us a lesson in pistol shooting!" he scowled scornfully. "Go ahead, kid, shoot!"

Hogan, with the .45 in both hands, ripped off a clip into the silhouette target, drilling a group into the heart you could cover with the palm of one hand. Red-faced, the Range Officer turned on his heel and stalked away. Hogan really was a cowboy who learned to shoot on a Wyoming cattle ranch. His two-handed pistol style was the same exact one used by the FBI in training today. Hogan was decades ahead of his time, only he never lived long enough to crack off a shot in combat.

Our truck convoy churned and skidded through the mud for a mile to the edge of a clearing where we dug in for the night.

The clearing gave our 75mm howitzers an obstacle-free opening through which to fire. Within minutes we had our four guns set up in line, ready to shoot. Gun crews stacked clover leaves of ammo in small adjacent pits and everyone dug a foxhole for the night.

The communications sergeant, Jim Von Gremp, and I slid into the company command post with two radios to established contact with our team of forward observers, a lieutenant and a corporal well out on the rim of the infantry line. Captain Johnston had our machine guns and Browning automatic rifles set up on the flanks in case the Japanese attempted to break into our position.

The radios crackled "Fire mission!" Von Gremp yelled. Gunners jumped to their cannons.

Captain Johnston slid into the pit and grabbed the radio receiver "What've you got? Uh-huh. Yeah."

He ordered one gun to load up with a smoke shell, gave the range and deflection.

The gun crew slammed a shell into the breech "Ready to fire!" the crew chief called out.

"Fire!" Captain Johnston then handed the hand set over to Eddie Springmeyer, a fire control corporal. "O.K., son. It's all yours."

Springmeyer clipped on a head set and was in direct contact with the Forward OP.

"Up 200! Left 50! One round smoke!" Springmeyer called out, adjusting the single cannon to fire 200 yards farther out and 50 yards left of where the smoke shot landed. The other three guns in the battery swung in unison, following the correction. On a large drawing board, Eddie plotted the adjustment. The last one must have been close to the target. The final correction came down "Up fifty. High Explosive, quick fuse!" Eddie called out: "Battery, four rounds! Fire for effect!"

In a matter of seconds four guns sent 16 75mm shells

screaming off into the jungle. We heard the distant crump-crump as they landed.

"Jap machine gun." Eddie relayed the target to us "It's not firing any more."

One loader of a gun crew cut off a salute. "That's one for Hogan," he said.

But all that artillery action brought us some unwanted response. Just at dark, a Japanese 81mm mortar crew infiltrated and zeroed in on our position. Off somewhere in the coconut groves we heard the hollow "floomp" as a mortar shell went out of is tube. It exploded fifty yards in front of us. The next one hit about 25 yards behind, followed by a deafening crash near one of our gun emplacements. We knew they had the range and would send some more in. We hugged the earth in our fox holes, said our prayers and tensed up. Several whooshed in and exploded, making the ground shake and our ears ring. The last two came in and whumped into the ground so close they were almost within reach. Neither exploded. Either they hadn't been properly armed before firing or jungle moisture had taken its toll. They were duds. My feet told me to move quickly somewhere else for the night, but I didn't know exactly where those two duds were and I didn't want to kick one in the dark Still, it was a tense night knowing those two shells were only a whisker away and could conceivably go off any time. Luckily, no one in our company got nicked in the shelling.

When daylight came, I raised up and looked out. The tail fins of the two unexploded mortar shells were sticking out of the mud a few feet away. I promptly moved over 25 yards and dug a new fox hole, just in case.

The captain called Von Gremp to the command post dugout after breakfast and pointed out that the radios were operating fitfully in the dampness. He ordered a phone line be laid up the road to where our forward observers were dug in with the Sixth Infantry. Rain didn't seem to bother the telephones as much as the radios. Von Gremp was told to string the wire off the ground, up in the palm trees, so tanks or trucks wouldn't run over and break it.

Jim had worked for a phone company in Missouri before the war and was the only one in communications with experience in steel pole climbers, those big spikes that strap to the inside of each leg and can be jammed into a pole or tree. We watched from below as Jim ascended the first tree, secured by a leather belt that he shoved ahead as he moved upward. It was on-the-job training for the communications crew and Von Gremp was a good instructor.

Privates Livesy and Boles carried a huge drum of phone wire on a steel axle between them, peeling off wire as Jim climbed to string it up. My job was to walk ahead, rifle ready, scrutinizing the palm fronds to make sure the coconut trees were not occupied by Japanese with .256 Arisaka sniper rifles. In addition, we had several extra drums of phone wire in an accompanying 3/4 ton truck. The truck was armed with a 50 caliber anti-aircraft machine gun mounted on a steel pedestal directly behind the driver's seat. To make sure everything was operational, Fox Company machine gun sergeant Barnie Crosswise was driving the truck. His real name was something like Kauzukiewiecz, but nobody could pronounce it. Everybody in the battery, including the captain, called him Crosswise. Our wire detail was a formidable quintet.

If it hadn't been for the war, it would have been a glorious morning. There was a cool breeze, the sun was out, brilliant green coconut trees were silhouetted against the greenish blue jungle behind. Bright butterflies circled in the sunlight and a number of white parrots hooted at us from the palm branches. We had laid wire for perhaps a quarter mile when we heard the sound of an airplane engine and the sputter of machine gun fire. We all looked up at Von Gremp, hoping he could identify he commotion from his lofty perch in the upper reaches of a coconut palm. But his vision was obscured by palm branches and he looked down at us with concern. "What's that racket?" he yelled tensely.

"I think it's our planes taking off from Henderson Field," yelled machine gunner Crosswise, who also doubled as our company aircraft identification expert. "They are probably clearing their guns on takeoff to make sure they are working." We relaxed.

At this juncture, Von Gremp let out a scream from his high perch: "JAPS!"

A small, silver monoplane with unmistakable bright red circles under the wings came around a bend in the road at tree-top height, flaps down and machine guns chattering. Livesy, Boles and I dove into a roadside ditch. The Jap Zero mushed down the road at near-stall speed, fishtailing back and forth, picking targets of opportunity, for which we happened to qualify.

In a moment, the plane and the hail of machine gun fire had passed. Livesy, Boles and I stuck up our heads. "Anybody hit?"

Sergeant Crosswise slid out from beneath the truck where he had taken cover. "I'm O.K."

"You were supposed to be firing that machine gun!" I yelled.

"Didn't have time," Crosswise grinned, obvious glad to be alive.

It was then we heard an agonized moan. Von Gremp! We ran to where Jim was lying below the big coconut tree, holding his groin.

"You hit, Jimmy?"

He moaned louder and mumbled for us to take the steel climbers off his legs. We thought he was shot in the lower midsection until he explained through clenched teeth that when the Jap plane appeared, he simply pulled the spikes out of the tree and slid all the way down the trunk to the ground. Coconut trees have rough, corrugated bark and when Jim plummeted down, the bark shredded the cloth off the crotch of his pants and a lot of skin with it. Gently, we picked him up, Livesy and Crosswise

14

under his arms, Boles and I holding his legs. We deposited him carefully in the truck, then raced to the aid station where our Navy corpsman attended to his wounds. All Tony had to work with was Merthiolate, which had an alcohol base. When he started dabbing around Jim's torn groin we couldn't stand the awful moans and groans, so we left. On the way to the truck, Livesy said: "I think Von Gremp would rather have been hit by the Jap machine gun."

Anyhow, we had watched Von Gremp string wire and figured we knew how to use the climbers. So we went back to work. Boles finished hanging the wire in the palm trees. It was two days before Von Gremp, was able to limp back to duty. "Next time we string wire," he noted sourly, "We're gonna have somebody along who can identify the sound of Jap plane ... and make sure the 50 caliber machine gun is operating."

Chapter 2
War – Jungle Work

The shoes, tied by their laces to the straps on the khaki backpack, appeared brand new. This was the most obvious thing, other than the fact that the pack was on a soldier lying face down and dead. Leaning a little further out on the trail revealed another soldier, also dead. Recently dead. And ahead of him were the feet belonging to a third. From the fact that their rifles were still hanging over their shoulders on leather slings, it was obvious that they hit an ambush and went down in one burst. Where the burst came from had to be just ahead on the trail. Who fired the burst could also be just ahead. I signaled to the next Marine in the patrol that there were men down on the trail, possible enemy ahead and that I was moving forward, parallel to the trail, not on it. The Marine nodded and eased up to cover me.

Our eight-man patrol was assigned to check out the trails in thick jungle between our artillery position and the main line of resistance, 800 yards ahead. The Japanese had habit of quietly moving around or through defenses at night, putting out mines or setting up ambushes on jungle trails in areas they had been driven from earlier. At daybreak, we had heard sporadic fire beyond our defense line and assumed some enemy had infiltrated. Captain Johnston ordered a patrol to check out the trails near our area so we wouldn't get any unwelcome surprises.

Our patrol was following the rules to the letter. We were spread out in the thick green understory several paces apart. Being senior NCO, I was in the lead. The next man was about 15 steps behind but kept me in sight and I moved slow enough to keep him in view when I glanced back. The rest of the patrol was scattered back, each man keeping track of the man in front of him. Second in command brought up the rear. We maintained as much interval as possible. If we ran into trouble, only one or possibly two men could get hit at once. From what glimpses I had of the dead soldiers on the trail, they were walking bunched up, only a few steps apart, providing a good target.

Moving slowly from tree to tree, parallel to the trail, I paused where a pile of freshly cut palm fronds came into view. Palm fronds did not get cut on their own. Somebody had cut them. One thing we learned early about the enemy - they were experts at concealment. When on patrol, one had to keep alert to details - not only to sounds and movement, but anything out of place, like cut palm fronds or clumps of foliage. Most of us in the Marine Corps had been hunters in civilian life. We not only knew how to shoot accurately, but we were experienced in observing the terrain around us, seeing without being seen, quick to pick out anything which didn't look right.

From captured Japanese training manuals, our intelligence people determined that the enemy preferred to get us within a hundred yards, close as possible, so they wouldn't miss. Marine riflemen, on the other hand, didn't miss anyone within 300 yards if we could see them. The jungle on Guadalcanal, however, was dense and visibility usually short. Patrols often followed estab-

18

lished trails which made them vulnerable to ambush by any hidden enemy.

When I spotted the cut palm fronds, I moved silently parallel to the trail, flanking any possible problem. The Marine behind me eased forward where he could cover my butt, as I edged around the side of the pile. There was no movement, no sound. Carefully scrutinizing the jungle on all sides and above (sometimes Jap snipers climbed trees and fired from overhead) I eased closer to the back of the palm pile where there was some loose dirt and an entrance to a small gun pit. Rifle ready, I leaned over for a look under the palm branches. The pit was no longer inhabited. However, there were 50 or 60 brass cartridge cases from a Jap machine gun. The enemy had caught the soldiers up close, cut them down, then picked up their machine gun and left.

Not only was the first soldier carrying new shoes tied to his pack, but so were three others. The patrol leader, a staff sergeant by the stripes on his dungaree jacket, had a pair that looked like my size. I eased out of the brush, untied the shoes- size 9 1/2 D- stuck them in my pack and went back where I could watch. Within minutes, the other new shoes were gone, too. We needed them. The dead would never need them. I made note of where the soldiers were so they could be reported to Division Headquarters and notification sent to the Army which could then locate their missing patrol and recover the bodies for burial.

All this time we did not speak, but operated with hand signals. Even in dense jungle, sounds travel. The sound of a human voice is audible for dozens of yards. If there were enemy around, we were not about to make their job easier by revealing our presence. We felt sorry for the soldiers sprawled on the ground. They were dead as the result of poor training or poor leadership, or both. Had they been moving down the trail, spaced well apart, perhaps the staff sergeant might have been hit, but the rest of his squad would have probably survived to fight. We were trained to avoid bunching up which would offer the enemy an easy target. And we moved as silently as possible. If there were going to be any surprises, we wanted to be the suprisors, not the suprisees.

The Japanese largely traveled at night. They discovered early in the war that mass attacks under cover of darkness would often panic the enemy. We were trained to stick tight, stay cool,, listen and watch. Where possible, we selected a position where we could see objects at night silhouetted against the skyline. Anything up and moving was Japanese. We were dug in, motionless in our fox holes. If some activity was apparent in front of us, we ordered flares fired by either navy destroyers or mortar crews, flares which lit up the area like daylight. What we didn't do was fire random shots into the night. One of the best ways to get killed was to fire a rifle at suspected targets in the darkness. The enemy would promptly get a fix on the muzzle flash, hurl a grenade or creep in to stab or bayonet the defender. The enemy sometimes avoided immediate contact when infiltrating in the dark, moving through to set up ambushes or booby traps to inflict damage on unwary troops during the day.

On Guadalcanal they quite often sent in small groups to outflank or penetrate our outer defenses during darkness and quietly move to a road or a trail where they could set up an ambush. The fact that there might be no immediate enemy activity did not mean the quiet would continue. Like deer hunting, one remained extremely vigilant, assuming that there was a target or several targets nearby whether or not they were currently apparent.

Moving at night inside enemy lines was not the sole province of the Japanese. Edson's Raiders, an elite Marine unit, operated mainly behind the Japanese lines at night and wrought considerable damage. Also, a unit of 50 Fiji Scouts, native jungle warriors with Australian officers, spent much of their time infiltrating Japanese positions. We had regular contact with these highly-effective troops. The hazardous nature of raider activity required good communication between raiders and regular troops.

20

They usually left our main line of defense just at dark and emerged from the jungle days later at a pre-arranged point. With all the risks they ran, the last thing they needed was to get shot up by friendly fire.

For several days we were in a coconut grove that was fairly flat, a grove situated adjacent to the muddy coastal road that traversed the island, parallel to the north shore. Somebody patrolling the beach discovered a Jap two-man submarine on a nearby strip of sand and when we had time, most of us wandered over for a look. Essentially the sub was a large, manned torpedo with controls so it could be driven underwater into the side of a warship. It was a suicide device operated by two volunteers, probably very small in stature. The conning tower on the upper deck was so small, none of us could get down inside the craft, but we could look inside and see how the compact device was designed. Why this one was on the beach we could only guess. There had been some extensive naval battles in and around Guadalcanal with maybe 50 ships, both U.S. and Japanese lying on what was called "Iron Bottom Bay." That two-man sub may have missed its target and the crew ran it up on the sand. Another guess was that the two-man crew chickened out at the last minute and decided not to blow themselves up for the Emperor, instead ditched their craft on the beach, climbed out and left.

It was while in at this location that we were occasionally harassed by a big enemy artillery rifle known as "Pistol Pete." Rumor held that this long-range cannon was towed up and down the coast by truck and used to fire a few shells into Marine positions and then moved on so neither our artillery nor dive bombers could get a fix on its position. It fired at odd intervals, usually a night, just to keep us awake. It never did a whole lot of damage and some of its shells were duds, failing to explode, perhaps due to jungle dampness. As our forces drove up the coast and overran enemy positions, the word came down that Pistol Pete was captured. But the shells kept coming in. Turned out there were several Pistol Petes, not just one like we thought.

One afternoon, a long line of Army trucks rolled up and moved into the coconut grove directly across the road. It was an engineer company with orders to improve the muddy road vital to moving equipment and troops up the coast. These were all brand spanking new soldiers right off the boat, clean shaven and wearing crisp dungarees. And they were armed with the new eight-shot Garand semi-automatic rifles. We had heard about them, but when we went overseas, we were equipped with World War 1, five-shot, bolt action, 1903 model Springfields. Rumor had it that most of the new rifles, along with almost all new weapons, were being shipped to England for the invasion of France. This was the first time we had seen Garand rifles in the Pacific area. Some of our company immediately went over and made friends with the soldiers and inspected their rifles. To show how green these news troops were, they had their rifles stacked in parade ground clusters of four adjacent to where they were busy erecting their tents and unpacking equipment. From long habit, we kept our rifles always within reach, but these troops apparently thought they were in a quiet area. They didn't know yet that the Japanese didn't play by the rules.

Nothing they did escaped us. Nobody said anything, but we noticed when night came on and the soldiers bedded down in their big canvas tents- with cots, no less- they left their rifles stacked outside. For some time there was considerable activity over there with people moving around carrying flashlights, but eventually the engineer area grew dark and quiet. We didn't even see any sentries on watch. These guys thought the war was some-where else.

When it got light the next morning, there was considerable uproar over at the engineer camp. Apparently a large number of their new Garand rifles were missing! Their commanding officer came over to our area, red-faced and obviously angry, found our captain and began complaining loudly. Captain Johnston listened without expression, nodded and dismissed the Army guy; then he came over to us and announced quietly but firmly that he did not want to know who stole the Army rifles or where they went, but he would allow two hours for all that hardware to be stacked alongside the road. If it wasn't, our company would be given a shakedown and anyone found with a Garand would be charged with a theft of military supplies, an offense usually good for six years hard labor in the Naval Prison at Mare Island.

Captain Johnston had one more directive: "The commanding officer of the Army unit came over here last night to use our latrine because they didn't have one dug yet. He hung his .38 pistol and cartridge belt over a log and later discovered someone swiped the pistol out of its holster. I want that back with the rifles!"

This announcement elicited a hoot of laughter; but within an hour, the engineers got all their rifles back along with their captain's .38 pistol. We hated to part with the Garands, because they were excellent weapons, but it was plain we had to get along with the neighbors. We lived side-by-side with the Army unit for several days and they turned out to be a pretty nice bunch. One thing they had was a portable field kitchen at their bivouac and we found that we could slip into their breakfast chow line and get pancakes and syrup or scrambled eggs, no questions asked. Heck of an improvement over C-rations.

One reason for the midnight rifle acquisition, was the fact that some of our men were equipped with unreliable Reising submachine guns. These were small, light, compact weapons that fired a clip of .45 caliber cartridges, the same shells used in the Colt .45 automatic pistols and Thompson submachine guns. We had a few Thompsons in our company and they were superb weapons. Also, each squad had a Browning Automatic Rifle, better known as a BAR, an excellent piece of ordnance. Although fairly heavy, the Browning could fire shots singly or full automatic and put out a lot of lead in a short time. It was also very accurate. Our ground defenses were built around the BAR and water cooled Browning machine guns, old but reliable .30 caliber relics left over from World War I. Eventually, we were issued some newer air cooled .3O's, but the old liquid-cooled machine guns were still most dependable.

When we were in New Zealand, we all fired the Reising machine guns on the pistol range. They worked fairly well there under optimum conditions. They released a fast string of fire. But in the jungle they simply wouldn't work. They were spring-operated, and a speck of dirt would jam the action. Also, the jungle dampness caused them to rust overnight The guys who had them had to be continually cleaning and oiling them or they wouldn't shoot. Those of us with the Springfield 03's were thankful for our weapons. They didn't easily jam. If the operator could slam the bolt shut by muscle power, it would shoot no matter how wet or muddy. Furthermore, the Springfield was extremely accurate. It held just five shots in a clip, but it was dependable. The semiautomatic Garand provided a lot more firepower, but just hurling a lot of lead into the jungle didn't always insure destruction of the enemy.

Anyway, the engineers kept their Garands and we continued with our Springfield 03's and Reisings. We also had a couple of riot guns, 12 gauge pump shotguns, loaded with buckshot for use up close at night. This was a devastating weapon at short range but worthless if the enemy was over 50 yards away. Later in the war, we had some of our people equipped with new .30 caliber carbines, short, light weapons that were pretty accurate but fired a very small, light slug. Trouble with the carbine was, it had no great impact. A charging enemy could soak up a couple of rounds from the carbine and keep coming. If he got hit with the heavier .30-06 slug, he was usually upended and out of it, even if he wasn't killed outright.

We understood that the best weapons were going to equip the invasion force in England. Roosevelt, Churchill and Stalin had agreed to open up a second front in Europe, dispose of Hitler, and then turn attention to the Japanese. The Navy, however, and Army General Douglas MacArthur didn't believe in waiting for the war in Europe to end. We were moving across the Pacific, island by island, with whatever arms we had. One thing we did have was Navy backing for any of our landings. Navy firepower was awesome and once the Jap fleet was chased back to the Philippines, we had fairly easy sailing. Also, we eventually acquired control of the air. With those assets, the hand writing was on the bulkhead. One thing we were aware of, although we couldn't see it, our submarine fleet was wreaking terrible destruction on Japanese shipping. The Navy wisely concentrated our subs on merchant ships rather than warships with anti-submarine armament. Within three years, the Japanese merchant fleet was decimated. This prevented the enemy from re-supplying their troops and re-enforcing the islands we later invaded. We figured that maybe we were in contact with less than a fourth of the Jap Pacific ground forces. We simply by-passed them as we moved toward Japan. A large part of the Jap army sat out the war on remote islands, unable to move.

On Guadalcanal, however, we had no great superiority other than our training and esprit de corps. Most of the Jap fleet was intact, operating somewhere in the vicinity, and their air forces were over us every day. Our supply ships steamed into Guadalcanal Bay, unloaded rapidly and sailed out again, giving the enemy little time as possible to strike. In the jungle, we were only dimly aware of the great scheme of things. Our war existed mostly at short range, through the next river valley, over the next ridge, mainly what we could see with our own eyes. We knew that this campaign would be over when the last enemy position was overrun, when the last shot was fired and we were loaded on the troop transports heading for New Zealand. We had no thought of returning to the states. New Zealand would be rest enough, a base where we would fill in replacements, resupply and head for the next islands north.

Chapter 3
Luck Doesn't Hurt a Bit

As backup for the Sixth Regiment, we had occupied the brushy east ridge overlooking a twisting ribbon of blue named on maps as the Kokumbona River. That piece of steaming jungle real estate had been fought over for weeks and the stench of death was almost stifling. Near our position was a series of trenches and dugouts from where a large enemy force had obviously waged battle over time. In a small grassy plot behind was a burial ground, the graves marked by short, vertical slats - Shinto sticks - with Japanese writing on them. What caught our attention was a single cross in the middle of the burial slats. Apparently, one of those enemy soldiers had been a Christian and his comrades honored him with a cross when he was killed. A few of us stood and stared at that cross for some time, wondering about that soldier, his family back in Japan and the utter insanity of war itself.

Below the ridge, on the shore of the river, the Sixth Marines were attempting to cross over and establish a bridgehead behind our artillery barrages. They had probed across several times, but couldn't maintain control. Similarly, the Japanese had stormed across in several counterattacks, but were unable to dislodge the Marines. Nightly entertainment included English-speaking Japs screaming threats across the river like "Marine, you die!" or "Japanese soldiers drink Marine blood!" stuff which was supposed to terrify us.

Marines, in turn, yelled insults back such as "Hirohito is a saki-sucking ape!" to which the enraged Japs would reply: "Babe Ruth is ape!" only they called him "Babe Roose." They had some idea that insulting a famous baseball player was the most offensive epithet they could hurl.

Word came down that a massive Marine offensive was being planned, led off by a fleet of newly arrived Army B-24 bombers. Jump off time was 6 a.m. Our job would be to lay down a string of smoke shells on the Japanese positions at two minutes to six. The bombers would appear at 6 a.m., exactly two minutes later, using the smoke as a marker to blow the Japanese position to smithereens. The Sixth Marines would then storm across the river and tear the west shore from the stunned and bomb-battered Japanese, perhaps even move up and take the heights above.

It was a heck of a plan. At first light the next morning, everyone was tensed up for the big push. All three batteries of the 2nd Battalion, 10th Marines were zeroed in on the Jap position, guns loaded with smoke shells. At exactly two minutes to six, the order came down to fire. Twelve guns thundered and puffs of white smoke appeared all along the Japanese lines. Perfect job. Then we began to scan the skies for our bombers. Six o'clock came and went. The troops below were tensed to follow the bomber strike.

Five more minutes went by. No bombers. Then a gasp of dismay went through our lines. The smoke was slowly drifting across the Kokumbona River onto the Sixth Marines' position.

And then we heard the bombers taking off from Henderson Field. The vanguard of the proposed Marine attack frantically scrambled out of dugouts and foxholes, picked up machine guns and began to hightail it up the ridge toward us in trucks, in jeeps and on foot. As the curtain of smoke continued moving and drifted into our position, we joined the flight. When the bombers at last appeared, our whole side of the river was shrouded in smoke and the bombers unloaded their lethal cargo with extreme accuracy. Dozens of 500 lb. bombs crashed into the smoke curtain our troops had just abandoned on the dead run, blowing dirt, rocks and splintered trees sky high. There is an old saying: "Marines never retreat." Perhaps not; but in this instance, they executed a "strategic withdrawal" at a very high rate of speed.

The Japanese promptly waded across the river and occupied the Marine positions on the east shore. It took several days of hard fighting and hundreds of artillery shells to retake the abandoned line. We never did find out if there had been a communication screw-up or if somebody simply had a slow watch. Fortunately, we didn't lose anybody in the bombing. But from then on, we handled the ground war with a certain amount of skepticism, perhaps not fully justified, where joint air-ground operations were concerned.

Eventually, we battled back to our former position on the ridge, once again hurling shells into the jungle beyond the river on missions called in from our forward observers.

One evening, several of us were out tidying up the barbed wire around our machine guns when a trucker named Sloggett pulled up. "Hey!" he yelled. "Somebody wanna go with me down to the water hole and help me pick up a load of fresh water?"

In the steaming heat, potable water was a vital necessity, particularly water treated to eliminate bacteria. I walked over and vaulted into the seat alongside Sloggett, glad to be away from the barbed wire detail. It was a mile back to the road junction where the army had a series of big, portable canvas tanks set up to treat water. After purified with chemicals, the water was poured into 10-gallon Jerry cans and trucked to various units in the area. The minute I jumped in the truck, I remembered I had left my rifle leaning against a rock by the machine gun; but since we were headed a mile behind the lines in a safe area, I wasn't particularly concerned. Anyway, I noticed that Sloggett had his .30-03 Springfield jammed in a canvas case mounted alongside the truck steering wheel.

It was a quiet ride and nice to be away from the racket of artillery fire for awhile. We followed the muddy, tree-lined road down to the junction where eight or so huge canvas water tanks sat in the shade of a coconut grove. Oddly enough, there didn't seem to be anyone around as we pulled up. Sloggett had just put on the brakes, when a rifle shot from above and to the right ricocheted off the truck hood and howled into the trees. A second shot plowed into the truck seat, but we were already out of the truck and belly-down in the mud alongside the left front wheel. "Sniper! Sloggett hissed. One more shot banged into the truck body but we were on the side opposite the shooter and somewhat protected. I glanced up at Sloggett's rifle in the case.

"Get your rifle before that guy hits us!" I hissed.

"Get it yourself!" Sloggett hissed back.

To slip back up by the steering wheel would mean exposing my head and shoulders, a situation that could draw a bullet in the face. At that point, a staccato of shots rang out from the shrubbery nearby. A Jap rifle tumbled down and hit the ground. Three Army soldiers stepped into view.

"Thanks," one said. "We were waiting for that bugger. We got him."

Sloggett and I stood up. The dead sniper dangled from a rope high in an overlooking coconut tree. "What were we, bait?" Sloggett asked.

"Yeah, kinda," the soldier laughed. "We knew he was up there but not exactly in which tree. When he cracked off at you guys, we got a fix on him."

Sloggett and I hurriedly loaded our 20 10-gallon water cans and got out of there. "I didn't think we would have any trouble that far behind the lines," Sloggett said. "In this crummy war you can get killed anywhere." It was the first and last time I ever went anywhere without my rifle.

A few days later, a detail of us was sent down to the beach in a couple of trucks for supplies. While we were waiting our turn at the dock, we decided to take a walk down the beach and see what was happening along shore. An Army reconnaissance plane was droning out over the ocean, then swung inland at a fairly low altitude. Some white papers fluttered out of the plane. "Geez, they are dropping leaflets," somebody noted. There had been rumors that the army was trying to get the remaining Japanese to surrender, but without any measurable success. Those leaflets apparently didn't work, either. There was a volley of machine gun fire from the coconut trees, the plane began to smoke, wobbled out over the water, slanted down and smacked in with a geyser of foam. Somebody spied movement on the floating wreckage. The pilot had gotten out and was bobbing up and down in an inflated life jacket in the ocean. He waved a hand feebly once and then stopped moving.

"Hey, the pilot is alive!" somebody noted.

"Yeah, but look where he is. He's closer to the Japs than to us."

We watched for a couple of minutes, expecting a Navy small boat to come to his rescue, but nothing happened. The arm came up again. "The guy needs help," somebody commented.

There was nothing else to do. I jerked off my shoes, pants and shirt and hit the water. Another Marine I didn't know came in behind me but was smart enough to push a coconut log loose lying half in the water. "We can get him with this," the other guy said. We each hooked an arm over the log and started swimming toward the wreck, which was fast settling into the water.

The plane was maybe a quarter mile from where we launched and about 400 yards from the shore where the Japs still held control. As we swam toward the pilot, the thought kept occurring that it wouldn't take much for a few Japs in a rowboat to come out and finish off the pilot and the two of us with him. Also, we were rapidly getting within range of their machine guns. On top of that, the bay was a notorious hangout for sharks. We kept looking around for fins although we could have done little if a shark appeared. But nothing happened. We eventually towed the log to where the flier was drifting in his inflatable Mae West life vest. He was floating with his head hanging down. By this time the plane had sunk and there was just the pilot, the other Marine, the coconut log and myself.

When we got close, we could see blood all over the pilot's face from a big gash in his forehead. Apparently, when the plane piled in, he smacked his head on the control panel.

"Hey! You O.K.?" The other Marine yelled as we came up.

The pilot raised his head and looked around in a dazed fashion. He sort of focused on us and managed a weak grin. "Glad to see you guys," he mumbled.

"Are you shot up?" I asked.

"No… cut on my face… my ribs hurt." With that, he suddenly let go a whole string of profanity somehow connected with the idea that he should have been dropping bombs on the Japanese, not leaflets.

That seemed to exhaust him and he looked pretty sick. His head kept nodding down toward the water. The other Marine and I managed to get his head and arms draped across the log. Then we started swimming back. I fully expected a Jap machine gun to start spraying us, but nothing happened. It took us a little time, but we managed to drag him back to our own beach where a half dozen guys jumped in the water to carry him to dry land. Somebody ran to get a jeep ambulance and in a few minutes he was on his way to an aid station.

32

The other Marine and I sat down for a minute to get our breath back, put on our pants and shoes and left. I never did find out his name or the pilot's name. When I got back to the battalion area, Sergeant Von Gremp said, "I heard you and another guy went into the water to get a flier knocked down near the Jap lines."

"Yeah, we did."

"The word is, they are going to write you up for a citation."

"You mean a medal?"

"Yeah."

"Hey. How about that!"

But, as I thought about it, the idea seemed pretty dumb. We had not been under fire or anything like that. We simply swam out, got the guy and swam back.

As it turned out, nothing ever came of it. There was a lot of genuine heroic stuff going on in the jungle every day where people were getting shot up. Taking a swim for a downed pilot wasn't exactly heroic. Maybe the other Marine got something for rescuing the downed flier but it didn't create much of a stir in our outfit and was quickly forgotten.

* * * * * * * *

The First Division, which fought since the initial landing on August 7, had packed up and headed for home. "The First is going back to the states to sell war bonds," was the standard line. Command on Guadalcanal switched from Marine General Vandergrift to Army General Alexander Patch. This did not concern us a whole lot as we moved up the coast with the Sixth Regiment, pushing the remaining Japanese toward their last stand at Tasafaronga Point. We were back in the stifling, bug-filled coconut flats where our main concerns were huge land crabs, dysentery, malaria and the occasional infiltrating enemy. Our position was again at the edge of a clearing in the coconuts, a spot that offered a nearly unobstructed field of fire except for one huge tree, maybe eight feet in diameter with huge buttressed

33

roots, which loomed up in the middle. Every time we shifted our guns we had to be conscious of that obstacle so one of our shells didn't hit it on the way out and spew iron all over our position. Gunnery Sergeant John Young decided that tree was an unacceptable hazard and determined to get rid of it. Gunny Young was somewhat famous in that, at age 19, he was the youngest gunnery sergeant in the whole Marine Corps; but he was also an artillery genius. Our battalion commander, Col. Shell, assigned new officers to work alongside Young to absorb his artillery skills wherever possible.

It was a sizzling hot day, about 10 o'clock in the morning, when Young let it be known that he was getting rid of the big tree. All of us, Young included, had attended demolition school, but we were far from dynamite experts. Young requisitioned two crates of TNT from battalion headquarters and proceeded with his mission - to cut the tree trunk in half with dynamite. The jungle tree was a huge thing, at eight feet across the stump. Young set about lashing sticks of dynamite in a circle around the trunk. Nobody paid a lot of attention as he labored in the heat, stringing block after block in place. No one noticed that Young used both cases of dynamite, infinitely more than was needed. Then he rigged up a hand grenade for a detonator, tied a string to the grenade pin and slid into a shallow foxhole nearby and called out the usual warning: "Fire in the hole!"

We all took cover in whatever holes or pits were handy and waited. Young jerked the pin and the dynamite erupted with an ear-splitting boom. It was deafening. Pieces of tree trunk flew off in all directions. When the dust and smoke began to clear, several of us stalked over tensed and angry. All that was left was a jumbled basin of loose dirt and bits of bark. We were stunned to find no trace of Gunnery Sergeant Young.

"My God!" somebody groaned in disbelief. "Young blew himself up with the tree!"

At that point some of the loose dirt began to move and up

from the debris came a dirty, disheveled but grinning gunnery sergeant. "I did it!" he exulted.

"What did you use?" somebody asked.

"Two cases of TNT," Young laughed. "I wanted to make sure the tree came down."

"Came down?" Sergeant Von Gremp shook his head. "You blew it clean off the island. With people like you around, I don't know if I'm gonna to live long enough to get killed by the Japanese."

* * * * * * * *

Land crabs, mentioned before, were about 12 inches in diameter, stayed out of sight in the daytime, but came out at night to scuttle through the dry leaves. They weren't dangerous to people, but they were an ugly nuisance. On the other hand, the infiltrating Japanese, crawling in under cover of darkness, were a real concern. They crept in on hands and knees, looking to blow up command posts or anything connected with the artillery, which was pounding them during the day. It was pitch dark in the jungle at night and sometimes they crawled along until they felt loose dirt from a foxhole or command pit. They would then feel around to find the edge of the hole, reach in carefully to see if it was occupied and if so, roll a hand grenade into the hole. At night we were acutely aware of any nearby sounds. We listened for movement and kept a sharp eye out, watching the sky above our holes for the appearance of a helmet. Japs wore what we called Pee-pot helmets which were distinct and easy to identify even at night. Anyway, anybody out at night who didn't identify himself was Japanese. We shot first and asked questions later. The trouble with shooting was that if there were more than one Jap, the muzzle flash gave away your position and could draw counter fire. Some Marines preferred to simply toss out a hand grenade or use their combat knives to avoid the flash.

It was one of those nights when the Japs were on the move. We could hear them slipping through the jungle understory, signaling to each other with empty cartridge cases. "Click! Click! Click!" A short distance away came an answering "Click! Click! Click!" They couldn't see us because we were below ground surface but we knew they were hunting for our foxholes. And we were tense.

Somehow, during all this, fatigue overcame me and I dozed off. What brought me wide awake was a trickle of dirt sliding into my fox hole and hitting my helmet. Somebody was on the rim of my hole! Next, I sensed fingers passing lightly over my face. Hoping the Jap would think I was dead, I didn't move a muscle, fearing he would feel the movement. I knew one of us was about to go. Before dark, my combat knife had been stuck in the side of my foxhole above my right hand and I quietly slid my fingers up to grip the handle. Tensed, with adrenalin flowing, I opened my eyes to get a quick fix on my assailant, ready to grab him by the shirt and jerk him into the hole where I could jam the knife into him.

What I saw were the long, skinny legs of a huge land crab dangling over the rim of my helmet, With a yell, I made a swipe at the crustacean which fell into the hole and went scuttling back and forth in the dark while I swung my knife, chopping away at the loathsome creature. Eventually, I smashed him and quiet returned.

"You, O.K. Sarge? Jerry Roybal whispered in a tight voice.
"Yeah."
"Did you get him?"
"It was a crummy land crab."
"What?" Another voice joined Roybal's.
"I said it was a big land crab."
The silence as broken by a chorus of laughs. "Sarge has declared war on land crabs," Springmeyer giggled.
"Ah, shut up!"
I didn't sleep the rest of the night. Morning came and with daylight, I picked up the now defunct land crab and hurled it

into the trees. Breakfast was a can of C Rations - meat and potato hash - and a sip of canteen water with the daily yellow Atabrine pill. The Atabrine was doled out a couple days as a time as medication to prevent malaria. That debilitating disease now afflicted 98% of the division. We took the bright yellow pills daily because that was what we were ordered to do. It was supposed to be a chemical substitute for quinine. All the quinine in the world came from the chinchona trees in the Philippines. When the Japs took the Philippines, they captured the world supply of natural quinine.

The story was that prior to our entry in WWII, U.S. intelligence infiltrated a spy into Germany where the quinine substitute, atabrine, was being manufactured by the I.G. Farben chemical company. Our agent stole the formula from the Germans, brought it back to the U.S. and U.S. pharmaceutical plants began making it. First and Second Division Marines were the first U.S. troops to use it. And the first to have almost 100% affliction of malaria. We found out much later that the clever Krauts let our spy swipe the formula without the key ingredient. All we were taking were tablets of yellow dye. We all turned yellow and we all got malaria.

The malaria symptoms of chills and fever came and went. Our medics had a limited supply of quinine, which they doled out when we were really critical with high fever and shakes. Dysentery was equally debilitating. We had a saying that you could diagnose jungle dysentery when you could poop through your shorts and not even leave a stain.

One night, doubled over with stomach cramps, I shuffled to one of the company latrines we had dug. They were deep trenches three feet wide and 12 feet long with a log suspended lengthwise over the top to sit on. As I got adjusted on the log, I became aware that another Marine was a short distance away, afflicted with the same problem. In the moonlight I made out the identity of my companion in distress.

"Captain Nielson," I muttered. "This is the fourth time I've been on this log tonight."

The old captain glanced my way and groaned: "Son, I wish I had been off this log four times tonight."

But the war went on, sick or not. Between malaria and dysentery, we were rapidly being reduced to skeletons. Our only consolation was that the Japanese were no doubt as sick or sicker than we were. With much of their transport sunk by the Navy, their medical supplies had been shut off for weeks. Although they controlled the entire world supply of quinine, they couldn't get it to their troops.

* * * * * * * *

We had been in the same location for several days, firing on Japanese positions up the coast, enemy strong points we couldn't see but we knew were getting hit by reports relayed from our forward observers. One night, the Japs staged a banzai attack up the coast and we laid into them with every gun that would fire. So did all the other artillery units. Our observers reported back that there were Japs piled up three tiers deep all over the shore. They ran straight into our stuff like Pickett's troops at Gettysburg. And with the same result. The odd thing was, they charged in three waves, each one getting completely cut down. When the third wave was demolished, the attack ended. There was no one left to charge.

We were drawing return enemy artillery and mortar fire although most of it was well off target, just nuisance stuff. We had a crew of local native volunteers, jungle people, helping us bring in ammunition and cartons of food. This was especially appreciated because we were losing our strength from disease. Those native people hated the Japs with a passion and they did not seem to be afflicted with all the local diseases.

Sergeant Von Gremp came over one morning and said we had a break in the phone line going up to the Forward Observation Post, either hit by artillery or cut by infiltrators. He said to follow the line, check it out, and fix the break. Things had been pretty quiet and I felt no particular concern. The map showed a small stream up ahead so I stuck my only bar of soap in my dungaree pocket in case I got a chance to take a bath, something we hadn't experienced for a week. I also hung a coil of phone wire and a portable field phone on a leather strap over my left shoulder, stuck pliers and electrical tape in my pocket. I hung my rifle over my right shoulder and pushed off.

It was a cool morning, I was relatively free of sickness and looked forward to the walk. The phone line, following the east-west road, was lying on the ground, but back in the trees, away from truck and tank traffic. Elements of the 164th Army Regiment were patrolling the road, which added a measure of security. Especially since they said they hadn't seen a live Jap in two days.

Near where the phone line crossed the stream, I found the break, spliced the wires, called in on the field phone and restored communications. I felt my job completed. For a few moments I stared at the clear stream, which looked quite inviting. I fished the bar of soap out of my pocket, peeled off my dungarees and waded out into the river. The water was cool, just knee deep, so I sat down and began soaping up. At that point an Army patrol of six men appeared on the bank and eyed me with some envy.

"Hey, fella! How about borrowing your soap?" one soldier yelled.

"Yeah, O.K." I stood up to wade back in as the soldiers scattered along the shore, hanging their clothes on the bushes. All of a sudden, three rapid shots rang out from an M1 Garand. One of the soldiers, about 20 yards up the bank, had spotted a pair of Jap split toed canvas shoes sticking out from under the shrubbery, leaned over, got a glimpse of a figure lying prone with a rifle and shot him through the middle of the back. I splashed to shore, jammed on my pants and took a look at the enemy sprawled in a growing puddle of blood. The sniper had been lying on his belly, watching, with his rifle ready to fire. Why he didn't shoot me in the river, I'll never know. Perhaps he was waiting to get all of us in the river. Perhaps he waited too long.

I buttoned up my pants in a hurry and got ready to shove off. "How about the soap?" the soldier with the Garand asked.

I tossed him the bar. "Thanks for saving my hide."

"Saved mine, too," he laughed.

Chapter 4
Meeting A General

It was the last gasp for the Japanese on Guadalcanal. They had a terrible time accepting defeat. Ever since 1936, when they invaded China, the Sons of Nippon had won every battle, every campaign. They were combat-hardened veterans. They had seen some tough fights such as in the Philippines and Wake Island, but they had run over the Chinese, the British at Singapore and the Dutch in the East Indies. And now this bunch of untried U.S. Marines was knocking their brains out in the Solomon Islands.

The Japanese didn't let go easy. They fought for every inch. They sacrificed dozens of ships and planes in the fight and thousands of ground troops. The stench of decomposing dead soldiers permeated the jungle and the beaches. But the enemy never gave up hope of gaining the island back. As our troops began driving up the coast toward the last Japanese stronghold near Tassafaronga Point, small enemy ships were slipping in at night to extricate as many sick and injured as possible and another attack task force, unknown to us, was being assembled farther north.

The U.S. forces, now under Army command, aimed to finish off the Guadalcanal campaign. It was determined that the Army's 132nd Regiment, backed by one company of light Marine artillery, would be transported by watercraft 18 miles up the shore behind the Jap lines and make a drive from the rear to pinch off any remaining Jap troops. Fox Battery was picked to accompany the Army.

It was broad daylight as our small flotilla of Higgins boats chugged down the coast past Tassafaronga Point and on toward Cape Esperance, the westernmost Japanese strong point on the island. We watched warily as miles of jungle, coconut trees and sand slipped past, wondering if we were going to draw Japanese artillery fire. Nothing happened. There was no sign of life along the shore, just rusting old wrecks of beached Japanese transports, small craft and even a couple of beached two-man submarines.

We knew that quiet was deceiving. We knew there were still enemy left among the trees and rock ledges watching us. And we knew we would very soon meet them. Our landing was, luckily, unopposed. The 132nd Regiment and Fox Battery got ashore with no casualties. We moved a few hundred yards inland and dug in for the night, planning to drive ahead at daylight. We were also prepared for any nighttime counter attack.

In addition to our battery and the 132nd, we also had a commando unit of 50 Fiji Island Scouts with two Australian officers. The Fijis were short, stocky warriors with tattoos on their faces that gave them a fierce look. They had bleached their high, fluffy hair, which came out orange in contrast to their dark brown faces, green shirts and shorts. Each one carried an Enfield rifle and a wicked-looking bush knife.They were a fearsome lot until they spoke. They spoke softly in precise English with a very British accent.

"Oh, I say. Could we prevail upon you for a cigarette, old

boy?"

Our first contact was an eye-opener. Some of the Marines yelled at their buddies: "Hey come over here and listen to these guys talk! You ain't gonna believe it!"

One thing about the Fiji Scouts: They were very, very good at what they did. Before we made this final landing, they had spent their time mainly inside the Japanese lines, picking their way through the jungle, pinpointing ammo dumps, headquarters units, and artillery batteries. These they mapped out and slipped back through the lines to provide our artillery with targets. Once they found out we would trade cigarettes for Jap flags and swords, they brought out considerable loot. Some of it with the blood not completely wiped off.

They had been operating for weeks in conjunction with U.S. forces and had not lost a single man, a tribute to their skill and their officers, a pair of very dedicated and very deadly Brits. Each officer carried a Webley pistol and a packsack full of dynamite. They were a force to be reckoned with.

However, with our patrol, they were team players. The Aussie officers informed the Army commander that it would be best if they went ahead on point. "Our men can smell the Japanese, don't you know," one Aussie explained. And that's how we moved down the coast: the Fijis in front, the 132nd and our peashooters trailing behind.

There was only sporadic resistance at first. We knew the Japs were ahead of us because we found abandoned supplies, but they kept falling back, except for some of their sick and wounded who set up an occasional ambush and determined to die fighting. We obliged them. As the 132nd moved ahead, we had the job of patrolling the area between them and our artillery team, coming up the coast at a slower pace.

One bright, sunshiny morning, we made a half mile loop into the coconut groves ahead, then cut out to the beach to walk back on the smooth sand. Resting among the trees in a cove, and half-hidden by palm fronds, was a Jap Zero in mint condition. Sometimes in the dogfights over Guadalcanal, the Jap pilots got so engrossed in their work they flew until they ran out of gas and then were forced to come down. This plane had apparently landed dead stick without damage on the packed sand. We immediately took possession of it in the name of international salvage.

There is nothing that a bunch of 19 and 20-year-old kids might enjoy much more than owning a genuine airplane and this one was a beauty. We climbed up on the wings and then squeezed into the cockpit, one man at a time. All of the ammo had been fired out of the machine guns so we couldn't play with the guns, but we wiggled the controls and made the ailerons and elevators go up and down. Then somebody said, "Hey, do you suppose this thing will run?"

We checked the gas tank and it was dry. Somebody got the bright idea that maybe we could find a can of jeep gas some place and get the Zero running so we could taxi it up and down the beach. There was no thought of trying to fly it. None of us had any flight training. Anyway, any Zero in the air would be promptly shot down by our own aircraft. But we thought it would be neat just to get it running. Boles, Roybal and somebody else went back up the beach looking for jeep gas while the rest of us played with our plane. In a few minutes they were back, but without any gas. They had the Fox Battery Executive Officer with them.

"Hey, look at what we found, sir!" I said. "We got us an airplane!"

"That's government property," the Exec announced. "Two of you guys guard it and the rest come back to the company area."

"Wait a minute, sir!" I started to argue. "We found this Zero. It belongs to us."

"It belongs to the United States Government, sergeant," the

Exec said somewhat testily. "Now get your butts back to the company. We've got a war to fight."

The whole thing seemed eminently unfair, I felt ticked off and confided my irritation to Corporal Roybal on the way back. "Look at it this way, Sarge," Roybal said. "We owned an airplane for about an hour, anyway. I bet nobody else in the whole Marine Corps ever owned a Zero." It was a one way to look at it.

The whole patrol kept moving eastward along the coast, Fijis in front, elements of the 132nd Regiment and our company headquarters unit next, the gunners and 75mm howitzers struggling behind. We paused at one point when the Fiji Scouts reported some Jap activity ahead, perhaps a chance to fire off our cannons. We had forward observers with the Fijis who radioed back and asked for a round of smoke so they could adjust the guns. We radioed to the battery to find a place where they could fire so they tugged the cannons to the beach and set up somewhere behind us. The question was: In all that jungle, what could we fire at in order to spot the explosion and adjust the guns to the target?

Up the shore a mile, a wooded point jutted out into the ocean. It was decided that everyone could see a shot on those point-forward observers, fire control people and the battery itself. We figured it out on the map, called down for one round of smoke and ordered the shot which went screaming up the coast toward the point and exploded in a cloud of white. The only thing was, one of our destroyers was patrolling the coast and appeared around that point exactly the same instant. The smoke shell blossomed a couple hundred yards off the ship's bow.

It became immediately apparent that the destroyer crew thought it was being fired upon by the Japanese. Their gun turrets swung around and we all dove for a cover while our radio operator frantically tried to make contact and explain the mistake. The destroyer let go a three-shell salvo that came screaming inland, just over our heads and exploded in the coconut trees.

This was followed by two more salvos that blew palm trees to shreds and had Marines running and burrowing into the sand for dear life. The radio operator finally got through and called off the barrage and we all tip-toed out of the trees intact but somewhat shaken. Luckily, no one got hit, but it was a tense few minutes.

That misadventure turned out to be the only time we fired our howitzers on the entire patrol. We dragged them all 18 miles down the coast and never fired them again. So much for that part of the grand strategy.

We kept moving down the coast with the Fiji Islanders and the 132nd. At about mile nine, we received a radio message that a Japanese task force with several troop transports had been spotted heading for Cape Esperance, sliding up behind Florida Island in an apparent last attempt to reinforce the garrison. It was believed they would land on the sand beach where we were dug in so we spread out along the shore, lay several strings of barbed wire, set up our machine guns and waited for whatever assault might materialize. We recognized that our best bet was to catch them in the surf before they got their feet on solid ground. Before dark, we loaded up with extra ammo and extra grenades. We were prepared to extend them a warm greeting.

Night came, pitch black and almost silent with the waves gently lapping on the sandy beach. Sometime after midnight, there was the sound of ships' engines in the night. We tensed up and waited. The darkness was split by blinding flashes of naval gunfire as the Jap task force came around behind Savo Island and ran smack into our destroyers. The volleys of guns and the crash of shells was accompanied by huge explosions and glowing fires that lit up the bay as the transports took hits, flamed up and began to discharge their frantic troops. Hundreds of Japs scaled down cargo nets into dozens of small, eight-man, flat bottom landing craft. Paddles flailing, the enemy headed toward us as flares lit the scene like daylight. We gripped our rifles,

46

watching the approaching mass of small boats.

Suddenly the night was rent by searchlight beams as a fleet of U.S. torpedo boats ripped into the landing craft. Machine guns chattering, the torpedo craft zigzagged back and forth, strafing and running over the Japs and smashing their craft to matchwood. In less than an hour it was all over and not a single Jap landing craft made it to the beach. We never knew who those sailors were on the torpedo boats but they did an incredible job.

As daylight came, the entire bay was littered with pieces of paddleboats and the bodies of hundreds of dead Japanese soldiers. And sharks. We watched in awe as dozens of sharks churned and thrashed through the mass of floating dead, tearing them to shreds. A few Marines shot some close-in sharks which, in turn, were immediately torn apart by the other sharks. It took a strong stomach to watch that mess. Eventually, we packed our gear and got moving down the coast again.

One problem we recognized as our column snaked its way east: Although we had scouts out, we were vulnerable on the flanks and it would be easy for Japs to come around behind us. Which, at one point, they did.

We were perhaps 10 miles down the coast toward our objective when a communications crew was cut off. They had been laying a phone line behind, following us from Cape Esperance where a command post had been set up. A Jap patrol had gotten behind us, cut the line and was following it, apparently hoping to locate and kill the communications team. Our guys were alert, however, spotted their pursuers, moved to a wooded ridge away from the phone line and called in on their radio.

The radioman reported in a hoarse whisper that the Jap patrol was milling around the phone wire between them and us. "We are setting up a defense for the night in case they figure out where we are. It is too dangerous to talk any further. Over and out." That was their last communication.

Morning came and there was no sign of the wire team. No word by radio, either. Nothing. By eight o'clock, Lt. Osbourn expressed his concern. "We've got to find out what happened to the wire team," he said to Sergeant Von Gremp. "Send a patrol back and see what happened."

"Who'll I send? We're short handed already."

The Lieutenant looked around. "Send Cary." Obviously, I was more expendable than any of the better-trained communications people. He walked away,

"Oh, hooray," I said sarcastically "I've gotta go alone hunting for those guys who might be dead already. Not even a get away man to report back if I get nailed."

Springmeyer and Roybal grinned and made obscene gestures as I picked up several extra clips of .30 caliber ammo, stuck two grenades in the pockets of my dungarees, nodded, and started off. "Have nice trip," Springmeyer quipped as he waved goodbye.

The trail back threaded through a combination of jungle and coconut groves. The coconut plantations were nice because visibility was good. Very carefully I moved along, stopping at each bend in the trail to study the territory ahead. The trail brought me to a small, thatch-roofed village that appeared deserted except for a few scrawny chickens picking about. It was almost too quiet. I had feeling that a whole company of Japanese could be watching from the village. Still, the phone wire ran between the thatched huts. There was no other way. After a few minutes and seeing no movement, I eased to the nearest hut, rifle ready. Still no movement, except the chickens. Slowly I moved to the doorway and peered inside. It was empty other than a few woven mats and a shelf just below eye level that had what appeared to be some small replicas of painted heads. As I got up close, I realized with a shock that those were real heads. Then I recalled being briefed on these people, some of whom skinned out the heads of their dead relatives and shrank the skin over clay forms. They did the same thing to their enemies, it was said.

48

The heads were painted and had small seashells stuck in the eye sockets. I slowly backed out of the hut and decided to circle the village instead of going through it. I didn't know where the people were who formerly lived there but I didn't particularly want to meet them.

A couple more miles of following the phone wire, I came to a small steam and stopped. The wire went into the water and came up the other side. Obviously, if the Japanese were following the wire, they would eventually appear. Or, if our wire team was coming in, they would also be following the wire. I found cover in a thicket alongside the trail and stretched out to watch. Laying down was easy because like everyone else, I was half sick with malaria and dysentery.

I have no idea how long I lay there because I dozed off. What brought me awake was a burning sensation across my back. I jerked upright and swatted at a mass of reddish brown ants swarming on my dungarees. Somehow, I had lain in their path and as they marched over my back, they began removing little pieces of my epidermis. I yanked off my dungaree jacket and shook off the insects, moved a few yards to the left and again stretched out; but not for long. The sound of movement in the brush across the stream caused me to loosen up a hand grenade and slip off the rifle safety.

Even before they came into view on the stream bank, I knew they were our people. They were swearing up a storm. In English. They broke out of the jungle and began wading across the stream, looking to see where the wire emerged. Not one of them spotted me lying in the shrubbery and I let them walk past. The last one was Boles and as he went by, I hurled a coconut that hit him square in the middle of the back. Boles let out a yell that must have been heard all the way to Tokyo. The whole group swung their rifles around, ready for a fight as I stepped out in the open.

This generated a surplus of profanity, particularly from

49

Boles who initially thought he had been shot. They said some awful things about me and made reference go my probable ancestry. I thought it was pretty funny but I was also relieved they had come through the night O.K. And it was a relief that it was they who came down the trail and not a Jap patrol. We lit up cigarettes and they related how they laid out on the jungle ridge all night, holding their breath, listening to the Japanese talking in the dark.

"We didn't get any sleep," Boles affirmed. "Luckily, we had moved away from the phone line and they were monkeying around with that. They had no idea we were right next to them."

"Listen," Livesy said. "They were so close we could hear those buggers breathing."

We trooped back to the company area and reported to Captain Johnston. The one thing we knew was that there were still effective Japanese around. On all sides of us and it was only a matter of time until it hit the fan.

The 132nd and our company kept moving up the coast, a few hundred yards at a time. It was a struggle because we were all half sick with malaria and dysentery and we were tugging and bulling those 75 pack howitzers plus cloverleaves of shells down the trail. We never did find a target to use them on. The Fiji Scouts, a lot better in this climate than we, stayed out in front. The Aussie officers reported enemy contact every day and warned that sooner or later we would be in a fire fight. By radio, we learned the main body of Army and Marines had stalled out at Tassafaronga Point, waiting for us to show up. It was up to us to make the contact. We also found out a lot of the enemy had been evacuated at night by boat, but how many were left, nobody knew.

The day after the phone line emergency, some of our men on patrol picked up a Jap prisoner. This was a fairly unusual occurrence since few Japanese would ever surrender. Also, we seldom took prisoners. But the word had come down that the high command wanted any prisoners we could get in order to gain information on the remaining enemy strength. There was quite a lot of excitement when they brought the prisoner down to the beach. He was a skinny little guy and they had left him only his underwear so he couldn't hide any weapons. And he was scared half to death. His eyes rolled around like he expected to get shot any minute.

One of the guys gave him a drink of water and tried to calm him down. Somebody radioed Tassafaronga Point with the information. The reply was that a Higgins Boat was being dispatched immediately to pick up the prisoner. About then, Chick McAdams came roaring down out of the coconut grove. Chick was a noisy blowhard from Texas that nobody much liked. He talked a heck of a war but every time we got into a tight situation, he was usually nowhere to be found. In any event, he came storming up, aimed his rifle at the little Jap and yelled "Git outta the way. Ah'm gonna shoot me this here Jap."

"Aw, button up, McAdams," somebody in the patrol snarled. "We had a lot of trouble getting this guy down here and you ain't gonna do anything to him."

McAdams persisted, waving his .30-03 and making threatening noises that had the prisoner shaking all over.

As the senior NCO on the scene, it was my problem. I stepped up to McAdams: "O.K., you want to do some killing, Chick, but I'm sure you want it all fair and square." I pulled my combat knife out of its sheath. "I'll give this Jap my knife and you take your knife and both of you go at it right here on the beach, even up. That's the way you would want to fight, isn't it, McAdms? Even up. Fair and square?"

This got an agreeable laugh from the guards who insisted McAdams and the Jap go at it with knives. Chick got a little pale in the face, looked around and snarled something about we being a bunch of wise guys; but he buttoned up and backed away. He wasn't called "chicken" for nothing.

In any event, the Higgins boat showed up and churned into the beach. We hustled the Jap on board and waved goodbye to the three Navy crewmen. The boat was getting underway when there was a loud bang and a puff of smoke. And the boat stopped. A crewman stuck his head over the gunwale and yelled: "Geez, the little guy got hold of a hand grenade and blew himself up!" So much for taking prisoners.

The following morning, at daybreak, we were packing up our gear to move out when a Jap Nambu machine gun and some rifles cut loose right in the middle of our position. Apparently a Japanese squad had slipped in during the night, set up on the rim of our perimeter and cut loose when we were up and moving about. The men closest to the machine gun happened to be the Fiji Scouts and six went down in the first burst. I shared a double foxhole with Myron Fleckenstein who was armed with a submachine gun. The trouble was, Myron had disassembled the gun to clean it and had parts scattered on his poncho in the bottom of the hole. "For cripes sake, Fleck," I whispered, "Get that thing back together. They may try to run over us."

We had no way of knowing how big a bunch we were up against, so I eased up on my elbows to peer around a coconut tree for a better look. At that, the Jap swung the machine gun around and blew a stack of splinters out of the coconut tree a foot over my head. I ducked down and waited. I hadn't seen any others so I assumed it was a small force. There was a burst of rifle fire, a couple of grenades went off and the machine gun quit. Myron had his gun together and we raised up for another look. There were only a half dozen Japs, all dead. We walked over and offered our condolences to the Fijis who were laying out their dead comrades. In 30 minutes, we were on the way again, the squad of very somber Fiji Scouts out in front.

Two more days and a scattering of fire and we finally linked up with the main force near Tassafaronga Point. We were tired, dirty and completely beat from malaria, dysentery, the heat and lack of sleep. The men from the 132nd flopped in the shade along the south side of the road and we flopped in the shade on the north side, waiting for somebody to show up who knew what we were supposed to do next.

At this point, several Jeeps pulled up. The lead Jeep had two stars painted on the bumper. An officer in starched Army khaki and a shiny pistol in a holster climbed out and went over to the men of the 132nd. They scrambled to attention and saluted sharply. Then the officer turned around and we saw the two stars on his helmet. A Major General. We knew immediately it wasn't Marine General Alexander Vandergrift, so we didn't move although we probably should have. The Army general looked at us lying in the shade, not moving, and walked over. "What outfit?" he asked, an edge in his voice.

"Second Division Marines, sir," I said without moving.

He eyed us intently for a few seconds. "Well, good job!" he snapped, climbed in his jeep and drove off.

Some of the Army guys came running across the road. "You know who that was?" they yelped.

"No. Who?"

"That was General Patch!" one soldier gasped. "He's the Commanding General!"

"Well, he ain't our general," said one of the Marines. And we stayed sprawled out until the trucks came to pick us up.

Chapter 5
Mail Call

With the last organized resistance finished on Guadalcanal, we were trucked to a bivouac in a clean coconut grove where the air was relatively fresh and the stench of death a memory. We had time to bathe and shave, do our laundry and eat something beside C-Rations. The cooks did their best with canned corned beef, powdered potatoes, canned vegetables, pancakes and bacon, cheese and ham sandwiches with real bread and, suddenly, a lot of canned fruit.

The canned fruit was through courtesy of a Jap air raid. There were a dozen Jap bombers came in one night to hit the airfield and got slightly disconcerted when our anti-aircraft batteries opened up. One load of bombs smacked next to the regimental storage tents back toward the beach where the supply people were hoarding canned fruit for their own benefit. Dozens of gallon tins were punctured and supply had to get rid of them immediately. So every unit in the regiment, including ours, got a truckload of canned fruit.

Our scrambled eggs for breakfast were still made out of powdered eggs that had a tendency to get kind of watery and green, but we ate them anyway. And they were relatively bacteria-free. Some real bacon showed up, a nice addition to the eggs.

And we got treated water, which slowed down the incidence of dysentery. Most of the malaria cases were brought under control and Tony, our corpsman, doctored our tropical ulcers and jungle rot. Ulcers occurred with any type of an injury - bug bite, scratch or cut. Surface injuries simply would not heal in the jungle. Instead, they festered, became ulcerated and bore into the flesh. I had a hole in my left calf where a sharp stick had punctured the skin and by the time it was treated, the injury had ulcerated three-fourths of an inch deep into the muscle. In addition, constant wet feet and the steamy, 100-degree heat had created cases of jungle rot, which were like super-virulent attacks of athlete's foot. Even though I washed out and put on fresh socks every day, my feet were swollen, split, peeling and bloody. I had a lot of company in F Battery.

Tony had us soak our feet in helmets filled with gentian violet to kill the bacteria. This made everybody's feet purple, but it seemed to dry up some of the jungle rot. Also, we poured sulfa powder into the holes created by tropical ulcers and things began to slowly improve. On the morale side, mail came in a bunch. The first letter I read was from dad and it cracked me up. I was laughing so hard, the rest of the squad wanted to know what was so doggone funny,

"My father informs me that the U. S. Air Force sent him a formal letter to the effect that if I did not report for duty in Chicago they were sending the FBI after me."

"The Air Force?"

It really was a funny story. When the Japs attacked Pearl Harbor, I headed for Chicago with two of my buddies, Jack Darkins and Bob Rogers, to join the Air Force. We all three had

56

two years of college, an Air Force requirement. Our intent was to fly fighter planes, in the tradition of America's Eddie Rickenbacher, France's Rene Fonck, and Germany's Red Baron, all aces from World War I.

The Air Force recruiting office was on the Fourth Floor of the Federal Building in Chicago and at 10 a.m. there was already a lengthy line of young men eager to become pilots. We finally got to the front of the line, filled out our enlistment papers, received physical exams, took an oath to the Air Force and were ready to start flying.

"O.K., you are now in the Air Force," the enlisting officer announced. "However, we are so jammed up with volunteers that you will have to go home and wait until we call you." "How long?" somebody asked.

"Well, it could be six weeks or several months."

That was a definite let down. We wanted to get going and avenge Pearl Harbor right now. On the way downstairs in the Federal Building, we went past the Marine recruiting office. A fat sergeant with a cigar in his mouth was sitting at a manual typewriter. There was a short line. I stepped up and asked: "How do you get in the Marine Air Force."

"Right here, Mac" that fat liar asserted. (I found out later that flying cadets had to go through Navy flight training and then could opt for a Marine air wing after graduation). But the sergeant sounded like he knew what he was talking about.

"How quick can I go?" I asked.

"Right now."

"Hey, guys," I yelled at Rogers and Darkins. "Let's sign up here. These guys will take us right away."

"We're already in the Air Force," Darkins pointed out. "We took the oath."

"The Army Air Force is never going to get in this war," I retorted, and promptly signed up with the fat sergeant. He pointed a stubby finger at a door. I went in and took my second physical of the day and signed up to leave for San Diego the next morning by train.

Rogers and Darkins were skeptical of this project but I was hot to go. "I'll be back from the war before you guys finish basic training," I predicted.

Thus it was that the next day I shipped out by train for boot camp at San Diego. Rogers and Darkins were called up two weeks later and really did go into the Air Force, Darkins as a bombardier flying over Europe and Rogers as a pilot in Air Transport. I went to boot camp where I immediately notified the drill sergeant that I had signed up for the Marine Air Corps. "That's nice," he said, dryly.

Eight weeks later, with basic training completed, our platoon from boot camp, along with a lot of others, was lined up on the parade ground. An officer was calling off names and assigning groups of six to a dozen to various ground units.

My name was called off as being assigned to Fox Battery, Second Battalion, Tenth Marines and I could see right away a gross error had occurred. I stepped quickly out of ranks and approached our drill instructor. "Sergeant," I said as firmly as I could. "What about the Marine Air Corps?"

"You keep lookin' up, kid, and you'll see it flyin' over," he replied.

And that was as close as I got to flying in the Marine Corps.

Dad's letter clearly indicated that the Air Force had no idea I was in the Marine Corps over on Guadalcanal. As far as they were concerned, I had failed to report for duty on time and in the Chicago office they were more than a little irritated. The letter concluded by saying that if I didn't report promptly, they were going to send the FBI after me.

It all seemed quite entertaining to my squad. "What are you going to do?" Springmeyer asked.

"I'm going to write back and suggest that if the FBI wants to come get me, I'll be glad to report to the Air Force in Chicago." I don't know exactly what reply dad gave them, but there were no more threatening letters.

Along with letters from home, a lot of us got newspapers sent by our folks. It was fun looking at the December editions with Christmas advertisements, seeing what was the latest thing to buy, what was available in the stores. We looked especially at the car ads, all of them for used cars because nobody was making new cars during the war. A lot of stuff required ration stamps. It looked like about everything was rationed - gasoline, tires, batteries, everything. Meat was rationed. So was butter. There were newspaper stories about aluminum drives by the Boy Scouts, teams of youngsters going around to collect old aluminum pots to be melted down and perhaps made into aircraft. There were teams of volunteers who were doing work for the Red Cross. And there were stories about other young men and women in uniform, where they were serving. There were also notices of young men who were killed in combat, some of whom we knew from school. We knew their families, their mothers and dads. The war as affecting a lot of people, not just a handful of Marines in the South Pacific.

Other than nightly air raids coming down from Bougainville, there was not much hostile activity on Guadalcanal. Patrols were still picking up stray enemy soldiers. Native Solomon islanders were quite valuable in this activity. Japanese troops, in their arrogance, had badly mistreated the Guadalcanal residents who reported the locations of any Japs they knew to be hiding out. Some of our patrols prowled through old Jap bivouacs and supply centers hunting for any junk which could be converted into trading goods. There was a brisk trade at the beach with Marines trading Jap junk to Navy shore parties. For instance: one silk Jap battle flag in good condition traded for a fifth of American whiskey or two cases of beer.

One of our guys came in from a patrol with a wind-up Japanese record player he found - one of those old Victrola-type units, along with some platters. The trouble was, the records were all in Japanese and we didn't understand any of it. Also, the sing-song music was not exactly our type. Then one day, a truck driver came back from picking up supplies on the beach and had swapped a Jap samurai sword to a sailor for a recording of Bing Crosby singing "White Christmas." We played that record over and over until it was nearly worn out.

There was an issue of fresh clothes and shoes and we were given time to go swimming in the lagoon opposite the airfield. When we didn't have anything better to do, we wandered over to Henderson Field, sat on coconut logs and watched the flights going out and coming back from raids on islands to the north. Some of the Grumman's and P-40's came back pretty badly shot up and had trouble landing. And sometimes the ground crews had to pull pilots out of the cockpit who were banged up.

When we could, we hung around the operations shack, listening to radio calls coming in: "This is Baker Three George!" the radio crackled. "Five minutes from landing. I've been hit and can't get my wheels down but I think I can make the airfield. Over!"

"Baker Three George this is control. Do not land on the airfield! Repeat: Do not land on the airfield! You'll roll up the steel matt...dump it in the ocean!"

There was a lot of swearing from the pilot but he came in over the trees, engine smoking and splattered his Grumman Wildcat into the lagoon. He was O.K. when they pulled him out.

Just getting planes in the air was often a problem. The ground crews were continually cannibalizing parts off the wrecks to keep the other planes flying. One day as we sat on the coconut logs, we witnessed an argument going on around a somewhat scarred up P-40. The pilot was standing on the wing waving his arms and yelling at an operations officer who was yelling back. The gist of the altercation was that the pilot did not think the P-40 would fly. The operations officer had an uncomfortable crew chief averring that the plane had been completely gone over and should fly. Finally, the pilot climbed into the cockpit, slammed the plastic cover shut over his head, revved up the engine and started down the steel mat runway. The engine did a lot of coughing and smoking as the plane was up on one wheel, up on the other wheel, but didn't get airborne.

There was still a lot of construction work going on at Henderson field. This particular runway was not finished. It was smoothed out and matted for a short distance. Beyond that was an area of coconut tree stumps, which were being bulldozed away. The P-40 bucked and snorted down the matted strip, failed to get airborne and plowed into the stumps at the end. There was a heck of a bang and a big cloud of dust. The nose stuck in the stumps and the tail came up, angling at the sky. At this point, the plastic cockpit cover was jerked back, the pilot popped up, slammed his helmet and goggles on the wing and climbed down. He was all right, but certainly madder than a hornet.

When he got within earshot, he yelled: "I told you that damn thing won't fly!" This time, nobody offered an argument.

* * * * * * * *

One of the hottest planes in service was the P-38, a large, twin-engine fighter that packed six machine guns plus a 20mm cannon in the nose. This plane was faster than anything else in the air and served the cause well over Guadalcanal. Early-on, when the Japs had a lot of airpower, they would send in 20 or 30 Zeros to mix it up with our fighters over Henderson Field, and then try to slip in a dozen or so twin-engine bombers to hit the airstrip. Whenever there was a scramble, the Grummans, P-40's and P-38's would get off, the P-38's climbing up almost out of sight. The Zeros would come in and tangle with a the Grumman and P-40's, but the P-38's would wait for the bombers. When those twin-engine Bettys came in low over the coconut trees, the P-38's came screaming down, each making a pass and each putting a bomber into the jungle or into the ocean. Once we watched 12 Jap bombers roar in, watched six P-38's make two passes each and saw all 12 enemy ships blow up or crash, the last one hit the ocean heading toward Tulagi. This was on top of a half dozen enemy fighters that went down smoking or blew up. When one of their planes got hit, we cheered like kids at a football game. When one of ours got hit, we just stood silent and prayed for the pilot to bail out O.K.

After the Tassafaronga episode, our little corner of the war was temporarily buttoned up, but the fly boys were still facing a lot of combat every day. Along with reading letters and newspapers from home, we spent considerable time playing cards, nickel-dime poker being the favorite game. Several of us were in a tent playing five card stud one evening, with another dozen or so Marines looking on, when Corporal Dees strolled in juggling a hand grenade. Dees was one of our forward observers and had more face-to-face acquaintanceship with Japs than most us. And also with grenades. He kept tossing the grenade in the air and catching it, making most of us nervous. Suddenly, it "slipped" out of his hand, rolled on the dirt floor and the the fuse went "pop!"

Hand grenades were equipped with a pin, like a cotter key, which held the firing mechanism in check. When the pin was pulled, the grenade still wouldn't explode until the spring-held arm on the side was released. When that happened, there was this "Pop!" and the thrower had five seconds to get rid of the grenade before it exploded. In combat, five seconds is a long time and to prevent the Japs from picking the grenade up and hurling it back, we first released the firing arm and counted a couple of seconds before throwing it. To get the time right, we armed the grenade, then counted: "One thousand one, one thousand two" and chucked it.

Dees, playing with the grenade, suddenly announced: "Hey guys, I accidentally pulled the pin out. Will somebody hold the firing arm down while I jam the pin back in?"

This got the immediate attention of everybody in the tent, knowing we had a potential live bomb in our midst. And then Dees muttered "Oops"! The grenade slipped out of his fingers and rolled across the dirt floor. At this point, eighteen Marines flew out of the tent by way of the doorway or under the side flaps. Dees simply sat on the edge of a cot laughing his head off. What he had done was unscrew the plug in the bottom of the grenade and remove all the powder before he walked in the tent. The grenade was a dud.

Of course, none of us diving for safety knew this. We just tried to put as much room as we could between this fragmentation bomb and ourselves. Naturally, there was no explosion, no bang. We cautiously returned to the tent finding Dees doubled over with hilarity, tears running down his face. Nobody else thought it was particularly funny and there were suggestions that maybe we ought to take Dees out, tie him to a tree and set a grenade off between his legs. Nobody did anything, of course; but from then on, we treated Dees like Typhoid Mary.

Orders finally came down for us to pack up and prepare to load aboard a group of transports at anchor in the harbor. Some of us promptly hopped truck rides to the new cemetery, quietly threaded our way between the crosses and found the names of people who had served with us. We saluted them and then went back to our units, were marched to Higgins boats and transported to the ships at anchor. We had to climb up the cargo nets we had climbed down a couple of months before, but now it was a much greater effort. In effect, we were a pretty scraggly bunch of skeletons. It was a superhuman chore just to climb up the cargo net to the deck of the transport above. When we finally crawled over the railing, most of us simply flopped on the steel deck and lay here, trying to get our breath back. I weighed in at the sick bay aboard ship, tipping the scales at 138 pounds. The day I had landed on Guadalcanal, two months before, I weighed 170. So much for life in the South Seas.

I don't remember the name of that troopship, but I think it was the Franklin. It carried a veteran crew who had been in and out of the Solomon Islands with supplies and personnel for months, particularly during the early days when the Japs had superior air power, lots of surface warships and submarines. The crew was a great bunch and they served up some excellent chow plus all the coffee we could drink, day or night. Marines manned the smaller deck guns on the Franklin - 50 caliber machine guns and 20mm pom-pom, twin-barreled anti-aircraft guns. Luckily, we didn't need either because we saw no enemy planes. We had an escort of a couple of destroyers that hung off the side, cruising back and forth, watching for submarines, none of which appeared, a circumstance which did not occasion any great disappointment.

In a few days we swung into the familiar port at Wellington, New Zealand, moved back up to our old camp at McKay's Crossing and prepared to go to town and renew old friendships. In-town transportation around Wellington was by tram - electric street cars - with a doorway in front where you got on, paid your fare, and another doorway at the back where you could hop off after signaling the conductor.

One afternoon, I hopped a tram, proudly wearing my new combat ribbon for Guadalcanal, and sat down alongside a man about 30 years old. He glanced at my ribbon and commented: "I see you've been up to the islands, Yank. Bloody rough go, eh?"

We talked a bit about the war and I kind of spread it on a little, feeling pretty good about what our division had done. While talking, I noticed a small bronze pin his lapel. All New Zealanders who were not on active military duty were in the Home Guard, armed and trained in case of an invasion. "Is that a Home Guard pin?" I asked, in my ignorance.

"Oh, no, Yank. That's my discharge button."

I should have quit right there, but I pursued it farther. "Oh, you were in the military?" I inquired.

"Quite right, Yank. Two years in combat against Jerry." Then he reached down and hitched up his pants, revealing an artificial right leg "Lost that one in Greece," he said quietly. I was stunned speechless and felt like an idiot. Somehow, I gained my feet, stumbled to the back of the tram and got off at the next corner, although it wasn't anywhere near where I was going. It was just too embarrassing sitting next to that guy who had seen a whole lot more combat than I had even thought of. I put the Guadalcanal ribbon in my pocket. And I was very careful after that, when talking with New Zealanders, not to open up my big mouth around people who had over two years experience in a war in which we were relative newcomers.

Chapter 6
The Great Kite Flying Extravaganza

The first member of the Second Battalion to fly a kite in New Zealand was Barnie Crosswise, our machine gun sergeant. It happened like this: Sunday afternoons at our battalion camp were largely devoted to doing the week's laundry. Individually. All the dirty clothes each Marine accumulated over the week were boiled in a cauldron of soapy water over the charcoal stove in each tent. Next, the clothes were pummeled with sections of wooden broom handle, rinsed, wrung out and hung to dry. Marines did the wringing in pairs, twisting each garment in opposite directions until most of the water dripped out. We washed everything except the pair of white under shorts, called "skivvy drawers" we were each wearing, which meant a whole battalion of Marines was parading around camp in white cotton under shorts.

The three hours it took for the clothes to dry were boring. To alleviate the boredom, Barnie Crosswise built a kite frame out of sticks, glued paper over it, made a tail from some rags and rigged it up with a ball of string he had purchased in Wellington. Like every kid who grew up during the Depression, Barnie knew how to rig a kite. And it looked like he was having such a great time flying his kite over the parade ground that about four dozen of us determined to build and fly kites the following week. Thus it was, on a subsequent sunshiny Sunday afternoon, there were more than 40 Marines in their skivvies out flying kites on the parade ground while another 300 or so, also in their under shorts, with nothing better to do, watched. Included were Marines from Dog and Easy companies who came over out of curiosity.

At other points on the parade ground, a couple of half-hearted softball games were in progress and a few Marines were tossing a football; but the kite-flying exercise drew the most interest. In the midst of this melee on the grassy field, attention was suddenly focused on the slow approach of several large, black limousines wending their way from the front gate up the hill toward where we were gathered on the parade ground.

These were some very impressive civilian vehicles and we assumed they must be transporting some very important passengers. All of the activity, except for the kites gyrating in the wind, came to a halt as about 400 scantily clad Marines focused in the approaching limos.

Eventually, the slow-moving motor caravan wound its way to the edge of the parade ground and braked to a stop. A couple of partially obscured faces stared out of the car windows. We stared back. There was no insignia on the limos, no stars denoting generals or admirals, so we knew we didn't have to come to attention or salute. We just stared. Finally, curiosity got the better of Crosswise, who happened to be closest to the road. He edged over toward the lead vehicle, still gripping the string on his gyrating airborne kite. As Barnie got within a few feet of the car, the window on the front passenger side was cranked down and the face of a woman, topped by a large flowered hat, appeared. Barnie went rigid, then leaned forward for a closer look, turned and yelled across the parade ground: "Migod! It's Eleanor Roosevelt!"

And so it was. The First Lady was on a tour of military bases in the South Pacific and had just come from lunch in Wellington with a number of important U.S. and New Zealand officials. Unfortunately, no one had warned our part of the Second Division camp that Mrs. Roosevelt was coming and we were as startled to get caught in our skivvy drawers as she apparently was to see us. The word later got around that she had come to see first hand the Marines who had conquered Guadalcanal, to meet, as the press labeled us, the "nation's fighters who had just destroyed some of Japan's finest troops." In our scanty Sunday attire, we were at loss as to what to do next. No words were exchanged and the First Lady did not get out of her car. The kites continued to whip back and forth overhead in the wind and 400 astonished Marines in their shorts continued to stare. Mrs. Roosevelt coolly scrutinized the motley assembly, surveyed the four dozen flying kites, cranked the window back up and waved the driver to hasten on. It was then that it dawned on us how we must have appeared.

Our worst fears were confirmed weeks later when we received clippings from newspapers back home describing the First Lady's visit to various South Pacific military bases. She had high praise for most of them but suggested that the Second Division Marine veterans of the Guadalcanal campaign might need to be placed in a special camp before returning to the United States, in order to provide them with needed training for normal life.

* * * * * * * *

On the heels of this fiasco, we got involved in a much more serious matter. Saturday nights, a lot of Second Division Marines regularly descended on Wellington to enjoy the sights and

69

find, if possible, female companionship. The Allied Service Club in Wellington, the equivalent of a USO Canteen, was a place where troops could get a good steak for half a buck, unlimited ice cream and dance with friendly hostesses. Of course we out-numbered the hostesses about 20 to 1, but it didn't stop anyone from trying to escort one home. Outside of a few friendly New Zealand troops who were sometimes home on leave, we had the place pretty much to ourselves. Except one night.

It so happened that part of the Pacific Fleet was in port and well over a hundred sailors were in the Service Club. As luck would have it, an Air Force unit on the way to Australia was also in port overnight and several score of them were in the Service Club along with the usual large number of Marines. It should be noted that every branch of the service - on the ground, on the water or in the air - figured it was the best ever assembled. We were all fiercely loyal to our respective branch and quick to take exception if criticism was uttered.

Just how it got started, no one was ever sure, but a dis-agreement occurred between the three branches in the Allied Service Club. The disagreement degenerated into an altercation and. this evolved into a full-fledged riot. All the MP's, Shore Police and civilian police in Wellington attempted to restore or-der. Before the riot ended, a lot of furniture in the Service Club was smashed and some of the windows broken. And a lot of Marines, sailors and soldiers wound up in custody. All leave was immediately cancelled and the entire Second Marine Division was confined to camp.

Eventually, the Air Force unit left for Australia and the fleet pulled out for duty elsewhere. Wellington returned to near normal. Only we were still confined to our camp at McKay's Crossing. After more than week went by, our battalion was as-sembled on a Friday afternoon on the parade ground. We were called to attention as the Battalion Commander, Col. G.R.E. Shell, marched out to address the assembly.

"Let me say I am deeply disappointed in the Marines of this command!" he roared. "Some of you were involved in that terrible mess in Wellington two weeks ago. That was a total disgrace - a disgrace to the Marine Corps and to men of this battalion!"

Colonel Shell glared at the ranks of very quiet and subdued Marines who stood sheepishly at attention. "All right! Division Command is going to allow limited leave, starting tomorrow, Saturday. Liberty will start at 12 noon and there will be a 10 p.m. curfew. Everybody will be back at this camp by 10 p.m." A ragged cheer went up from the battalion.

The Colonel paused and glared at us. "In no case will there be any more fighting in Wellington! You understand? No more fighting!" Col. Shell looked sharply at the assembled troops "You have to understand that the Air Force and the Navy are allies of ours…just like the British and the French!"

There was a whoop of laughter as Col. Shell turned on his heel and headed for the officer's mess.

Chapter 7
Social Revolution

Max was a Socialist. Indeed, much of New Zealand was Socialist. But Max was one of those real hard core, fire-eyed Marxists who could quote those two old frauds, Karl Marx and Nicolay Lenin, at length. He was a teacher at the University in Wellington, a teacher who received his monthly check from the government and thus had the idea that all, which is good and just in society, comes from government. Like most Socialists, he was forever preaching on its benefits and rewards and we went along with whatever he said although we thought he was full of poop. Most of us had experienced socialist professors in college back home and we understood the best way to handle them was to humor them, agree with them, get along and get the grade they awarded for cooperation. We were well aware that the few students with the temerity to question socialist teachers were immediately subject to lower grades or failure.

But, Max, being a teacher at the University, had daily contact with a lot of very young and good-looking female students, a number of whom frequented his house. This is where the Marine Corps came in. Like all red-blooded young men with active biological drives, we were on the trail of anything wearing skirts. Somehow, the word got around Fox Battery that Max's house was a hangout for young ladies and also, somehow, some of us got ourselves invited up there. Along with being agile, witty and romantic, we also were drawing overseas pay, which gave us considerable spending money, much of which was used for providing refreshments at Max's pad. A favorite beverage was Wattematta Beer, a high-octane brew that was sold for something like 30 cents a quart. We purchased the stuff in 12-bottle cases and hauled them up to Max's.

Max also owned a radio from which we gleaned bits of information about the state of the world, basically how the war was progressing. We heard some of the rousing speeches given by Winston Churchill, which we applauded at length, since his views on the war were similar to ours: kill the enemy.

Interesting enough, Max held Churchill in fairly high esteem although they were on opposite ends of the political spectrum. Perhaps it was the fact that the Japanese wing of the Tokyo-Rome-Berlin Axis was two islands away and advancing rapidly south when we arrived on the scene. Max was certainly not an exponent of capitalism, but he was most assuredly not in favor of being subject to the Japanese Emperor, either.

And Max was in the New Zealand Home Guard. They had an arrangement in New Zealand's military that all able-bodied men had to serve; but only volunteers had to serve overseas. Those who so chose could opt for the Home Guard and were required to fight only if the nation was invaded. New Zealand had been at war with the Germans since 1939 and most of their military volunteers were out of the country. In a way, this was a plus for the Second Marine Division because there was a dire shortage of eligible young men and we strove mightily to fill

74

that void. One more thing. Being in the Home Guard, Max trained with the other guardsmen and was armed. In his study at home was a Thompson .45 cal. submachine gun and clips of cartridges to fire through it. Something germane to this adventure.

Another thing: Along with a all the preaching about Karl Marx and his Socialist dreams, Max was big exponent of free love. The socialists, we were informed, believed very strongly in free love. That is, all relationships were open-ended. Even those who were married, like Max, were free to pursue other conquests if so desired. Max's wife Dorothy was a very pleasant woman, somewhat younger than Max and a trifle plump. She never did seem very comfortable about the matter when Max was expounding on free love, particularly about his exploits with female students at the University. He was almost obsessive about this which led some of us to wonder if maybe he didn't have a problem; but we enjoyed hanging out at his place and didn't openly question his stories or political ranting.

It was a great place to get way from the rigid discipline of camp life, kick up our heels and live like a civilian for an evening. In some respects, it was sort of a lonely hearts club. We were lonely, the young women of Wellington were lonely and we sort of solved a couple of problems at once. Some of the University women even cooked up snacks and brought them over to go with the beer, so a good time was had by all. This went on for several weeks: the beer parties and listening to Max's exploits with the women under his banner of free love.

Obviously, even a bunch of young capitalists like the Second Division Marines could see some benefit to this. And it was not long before it dawned on some of our people that Max's wife was also a Marxist and appeared to approve of free love. Thus a few of our compatriots began to romance Dorothy. We never knew how many, but one we knew was Corporal Ernie Strand. Ernie did not do any bragging about his activities with Max's wife, but we knew it was going on. Some Saturday nights when we were up there in a party mood and Max was not around, Ernie and Dorothy would vanish from the scene for awhile, only to appear somewhat later as if nothing was going on. Unlike Max, who liked to brag about his affairs, Dorothy was tight-lipped. And this went on for a few weeks.

However, Max began to sense that something was going on at his house when he wasn't home. Perhaps some snoopy neighbors were tipping him off or maybe some of the college girls turned snitch. In any event, Max began getting a little edgy when we were there, particularly when some of our comrades, like Ernie Strand, paid a lot of attention to Dorothy.

It so happened that one night Corporal Jerry Roybal, Ernie and I were in downtown Wellington having a nip at a pub called the Royal Oak, when Ernie's chemistry became active. "Hey, let's go up to Max's and see what's going on," he said.

We argued that there was no party scheduled for that night and there might not be any college women around. Ernie was insistent, however, that the place would be well populated with co-eds so we finally exited the Royal Oak and hopped a tramcar that delivered us near Max's domicile. On arrival it was immediately apparent that Ernie was dead wrong. There was no party there and no college girls. Max, we learned, was lecturing at the University and no one was there except Max's wife, which was just fine with Ernie. And with Dorothy, too.

After a couple of glasses of suds, Ernie and Dorothy got somewhat romantic and eventually drifted off to the bedroom. Jerry and I, with nothing better to do, listened to war news on the BBC station. We were involved in details of Erwin Rommel's impending defeat in Africa and Eisenhower's plans for invading Europe, when the front door flew open and Max strode in, fire in his eye.

"Where's Dorothy!" he bellowed.

For a guy who espoused free love at every turn, he was exhibiting all the characteristics of a very jealous husband.

Jerry and I shrugged and lied that we did not know. Max glared, strode to the bedroom door and tried the knob. Luckily, Ernie had the foresight to have locked the door when he and Dorothy went in. Max shook the knob, then banged on the door. "Dorothy, I know you're in there!" he bawled. "Come out of there this instant!"

There was total silence from the locked bedroom.

Next, Max stalked into his den and began to rummage around. Jerry and I were looking for a way to escape; but the trouble was, the front door was on the other side of the den. Max was between us and the door. Next moment, we were thoroughly alarmed to see Max coming out of his den, jamming a clip of.45 ammo into the submachine gun.

"Lookout Ernie!" Jerry yelled. "Max has a gun!"

Not only did it look bad for Ernie, but in his present state of mind we felt Max might make a clean sweep of all Marine personnel present. "Let's get outta here," Jerry muttered.

We darted from the living room into the only other room accessible, which was the kitchen. Like many homes in New Zealand, Max's house rested on the side of a very steep hill. The living room and bedroom hung out over the side of the hill. The den and the kitchen were partially dug into the hillside. There was only one out for Jerry and I. We climbed over the sink and went out the kitchen window onto the solid earth outside. From there we raced around the side of the house and came out below the bedroom. There was the creak of a window opening from above and Ernie came flying out, his pants draped over his arm. Luckily, there were some lilac bushes beneath the window, which helped break his fall. In a moment, the three of us were sprinting full tilt down the street and we didn't stop for several blocks, until we were sure there was no pursuit.

Under a street light, Ernie put his pants back on. "Migod!" he gasped. "Could you figure a guy like that who talked all the time about free love would get bent up about his wife making a little whoopee?"

We hopped a tram and went downtown where we finished up once again at the Royal Oak. There, with one more beer, we pondered our escape from possible homicide.

"I don't know much about Socialism," Ernie said, "but I know I'm not going up to Max's place any more."

And we never did.

Chapter 8
The Beer Hall Raid

It was time to pack up, move out and engage the Japanese
again. We knew this when the Battalion Commander, Col George
Richard Edward Shell assembled us all on the parade ground
and announced: "It is time to pack up, move out and engage the
Japanese again."

A roar of approval went up from the ranks. It had been
several months since we had returned to New Zealand after our
success on Guadalcanal. We had partied and played and gotten
into about all the trouble 18,000 high-octane Marines can get
into. We were frankly bored with training and playing war. At
one point we had been up in the mountains on the New Zealand
artillery range where we participated in joint maneuvers with a
Sherman tank battalion in sleet and snow, a heck of an arrangement since we were wearing our jungle dungarees tailored for
100 degrees in the shade.

The high point of this exercise in bone-chilling training for jungle combat was a simulated night attack when the tank unit got lost and came blundering through our bivouac in the dark. It was forbidden to show any lights so the tankers had no idea where we were until they began running over our tents, rousting out swearing artillerymen. In the middle of roaring tank engines and the stink of exhaust fumes, a series of screams punctuated the darkness. Not just ordinary screams, but very high decibel shrieks of total anguish. It was enough to bring out a number of flashlights, orders or not.

Corporal Ernie Devoe was screaming hysterically that his legs were cut off. As the tanks lumbered off into the darkness, several of us closed in on Ernie's screams. Our flashlights revealed only his torso, from the waist up, sticking out of the New Zealand muck. Indeed it was somewhat surprising that he could exhibit all that vocal energy when cut in half. Someone suggested that we get Ernie's upper half in a Jeep, then look for a his legs and haul everything to the aid station to see if anything could be done to piece him back together. While a couple of troopers began searching for his legs, two of us grabbed Ernie by the shoulders to lift his torso, an action which elicited another series of shrieks. The thing was, his torso wouldn't come up. It was strangely stuck. We gave an extra good heave and Ernie's body came out of the muck, revealing legs and all. The tank had run over him when he was asleep and jammed his legs out of sight into the soggy ground. He thought he had been dismembered, but other than some bad bruises, Ernie was pretty much intact.

Back at our camp at McKay's Crossing, we regrouped, doctored all the illnesses generated by the sleet and snow, and began packing equipment for boarding ship. The lightly wounded from Guadalcanal had returned to duty. The badly wounded had been shipped to Hawaii or the states. The dead had been honored and buried in the Marine cemetery on Guadalcanal. Replacements filled gaps in the ranks. The corpsmen had acquired an adequate emergency supply of quinine to whack malaria when it broke out. We engaged in tough calisthenics each morning and we hiked the ridges every afternoon. We were about back to top physical and mental state and ready to do battle.

However, the second announcement by our battalion commander took a lot of the enthusiasm out of the first. "We are going on full combat status the next two weeks!" he stated. (Yay!) "And the beer hall is closed as of right now. (Boo!) Battalion dismissed!"

A massive groan went up from 600 throats anticipating a dry and thirsty two weeks. "This is a rotten way to run a war," observed Sergeant Joe Zembles. His opinion met with almost universal agreement; but not everyone was consumed with doom and gloom.

"I think I've got it figured out," announced Machine Gun Sergeant Barney Crosswise.

"Figured what out?"

"How to get the beer."

"The beer hall is locked up tight and they have two armed sentries guarding it." The "they" referred to the ever-present arm of Marine Corps authority with which we were at odds with much of the time.

Zembles explained the impossible situation in detail: "The sentries are walking tours around and around, 24 hours, day and night. There is no way to get the door open and get the beer out."

"We don't go in the door," observed Crosswise. "We go in from underneath. See, the beer hall sits up on three-foot posts. We go in from below."

He beckoned and we followed him to the edge of the road. The beer hall was directly across from our company tent area. We could see the sentries walking their beat, one going around clockwise, the other going counter-clockwise.

"Once every couple of minutes," Crosswise pointed out, "the sentries are both on the far side of the building, passing each other. From there, they can't see our tent area for several seconds.

"See, we can get some guys underneath with a saw. We can cut a hole in the floor and take the cases of beer out from underneath."

"You're nuts," Zembles said.

"It takes a nut to figure it out," noted Sergeant Von Gremp. The ingenuity of the caper was breathtaking. It was possible. We needed only wait until dark.

At sunset, a dozen of us lounged by the tents, watching the beer hall across the road. The circling sentries, if they noticed us, gave no sign. They made their rounds, walking their four hours in utter boredom. As soon as the sentries were crossing on the opposite side of the hall, Crosswise, carrying a keyhole saw and a carpenter's saw led six others in a dash across the road. They slid out of sight under the building and the rest of us waited as darkness began to descend. The sentries passed by and then walked to the far side of the building again. Six grinning faces and six cases of beer suddenly appeared from under the edge of the beer hall. Six of us dashed over, grabbed the beer and sprinted back while more troops crawled underneath to help move the merchandise.

By carefully timing the circling sentries and working in total silence, over 250 cases of Lucky Lager were removed in two hours and neatly stacked by flashlight in front of the First Sergeant's tent. The entire roster of enlisted personnel was promptly assembled.

"We got to hide this stuff," the First Sergeant warned. "Everybody carry a case down to the ravine in the woods back of the mess hall. Some of you guys get shovels. What we don't drink tonight, we will bury in the woods for when we need it. Take a few bottles out for tonight if you want, but don't leave any bottles or any cartons lying around. We don't want to leave any evidence."

82

There were maybe six or eight Marines in the whole company who didn't drink beer, but the rest of us carried cases to the woods, then went back for the balance. This should have been enough beer to see us through the two-week emergency ahead; but, alas, Fox Battery simply could not stand prosperity. Particularly since we hadn't paid a cent for the beer. An awful lot of cases were opened that night and subsequently consumed in one heck of a party. When the bugle sounded reveille at daybreak, we were a mess.

The entire company assembled as usual on the parade ground, lined up in three ranks, more or less, in the morning mist. In a few instances, two men attempted to support a somewhat disabled third man by his arms. The First Sergeant was a real picture. He had his khaki fore-and-aft overseas cap on sideways. That is, instead of having the ridge running from front to back, it went across the top of his head, peaks over each ear. At this point, the officers shuffled down half awake from their huts and snapped to attention before us. They were not in on the raid and had no idea what had transpired during the night. Captain Johnston stepped forward and stared at us in the growing light. And stared some more, not believing what he was looking at.

The First Sergeant wobbled two steps forward, saluted sloppily and announced in a thick voice: "Foxsh Battery, all preshent an' accoun'ed for, shir!" at which point he broke out in an uncontrollable giggle.

It was probably the giggle that did it. Captain Johnston turned bright crimson. His eyes blazed and he bawled out: "Everyone back here in ranks in five minutes with rifles, canteens and full marching order. DISMISSED!"

There would be no breakfast. No lunch. We bustled around the tents, got our gear together, slid into our packs, buckled on our helmets, picked up our rifles and re-assembled on the parade ground. The Captain gave us: "RIGHT FACE! FORWARD MARCH!" and started up the road leading out of the division area. We curved up the side of the nearest mountain, up and up, at a very fast walk. Stragglers were grabbed and kicked or dragged along. We stopped every hour for a drink of water, but kept climbing until noon. At that point, we finished off our water and started back down. At 4 p.m. we filed silently into camp having had nothing but one canteen of water all day. Captain Johnston gave us a steely look as he dismissed us. But we were stone sober. Every blessed single one of us.

While we were gone, some of the junior officers went through our tents but found only a couple of empty Lucky Lager bottles. There was no contraband in sight and no one figured out how we got the beer. In addition, some officers inspected the beer hall, noted the door securely locked and nothing appeared amiss. Crosswise had swiped the beer cases from the middle of the stacks and the theft was not detected.

Months later we talked about that raid late at night in camps across the Pacific and in the mess halls of troop transports. The consensus was that there could still be a number of cases of American beer buried in the woods at McKay's Crossing unless some New Zealand sheep farmers made a lucky discovery after our battalion left.

It is probably safe to divulge details of the theft now, some six decades later. The statute of limitations has most certainly run out. Besides, perhaps the only three of the original beer hall commandos still alive are Von Gremp, Crosswise and I.

Chapter 9
An Atoll Called Tarawa

It was stinking hot in the hold of the troop transport Harris. As we plowed through the deep blue Pacific, heading north from New Zealand, Battalion Command had ordered us into the bowels of the ship to be briefed, one battery at a time, on the upcoming attack. Scuttlebutt had been circulating around the ship earlier that we were going to take back Wake Island, maybe hit Truk or one of the other Japanese strong points in the Pacific.

We knew vaguely that somewhere in the fleet our division commander, General Julian Smith, was conferring with Chief of Staff, Col. Merritt Edson, the ex-raider leader, plus all the regimental commanders. But now we would be privy to whatever our next objective would be and the bets were it would be a doozy. How much of a doozy we couldn't imagine.

Military Intelligence had put out a piece of fiction that we were boarding ship merely for maneuvers at New Zealand's Hawke Bay, across the North Island on the east coast. The Japanese didn't believe it and neither did a single Second Division Marine as we packed gear, struck our tents at McKay's Crossing and made ready to move out. The hundreds of Marines who had girlfriends in and around Wellington said their goodbyes and even the handful of deserters the MPs had been searching for showed up. One of these was Gook, our company barber.

Nobody called him by his real name. He was called Gook because he was one. That is, they couldn't seem to find anything he could do right. He was pleasant and easy to get along with but could not function in a military sense or handle military discipline. Command tried to make him into a Jeep driver and he promptly wrecked a Jeep. They tried to make him a Browning Automatic Rifle assistant gunner and he nearly killed the company commander. On Guadalcanal, he was cleaning a BAR, not a difficult procedure, but then got mixed up on re-loading. The rule was to slam the action home, which cocked the weapon, pull the trigger on the empty chamber and then insert a fresh clip of ammo. The BAR would be loaded but the chamber empty. When needed to fire, the action was jacked and the first shell in the clip would then be chambered and ready to go.

Gook got it backward. He inserted the clip, slammed the action home and pulled the trigger. The BAR fired. Not only that, but Gook had his finger hooked in the trigger guard and the whole clip went off, cutting a furrow of flying dirt and dust right behind the heels of Captain Johnston who was walking past the emplacement. Gook was immediately relieved of BAR duty. Finally, back in New Zealand, someone discovered Gook could cut hair and he became the company barber. They set him up with a barbershop in one corner of a storeroom and there he toiled happily day after day, clipping hair at 25 cents a customer.

One morning he was missing. Several clients, seeking a cut, found the clippers taken apart, the pieces on a table and a note pinned to the wall which said: "Clipper spring broke. Went to town to get new spring."

When he didn't show up after a couple of days, the MPs started looking for him and he was listed as AWOL. There was a running joke in the company whenever we couldn't locate somebody, "He went to town for a spring."

Anyway, we assumed, correctly, that Gook had moved in with a girlfriend in Wellington. There were hundreds of Marines with girlfriends in and around Wellington. Most eligible New Zealand men had been off fighting the Germans since 1939 and male companionship was in great demand. Maybe a dozen members of the Second Division found women with well-paying jobs who would engage in cohabitation. Gook vanished for a couple of months. Up until we were packing to go into combat.

Two days before we were going to board ship, Gook came back in time for noon chow, slipping into line with his mess kit like he'd never been away. "Hey, I hear we're moving out,' he said. "What's the mission?"

"Geez, Gook, where've you been? They've been hunting for you all over Wellington.'

"Couldn't find a spring to fit the clippers. Since I couldn't work, I figured I'd just as well stay in town," he laughed. "But where are we going?"

"Don't know, Gook. Some say Wake Island, some say Truk. Could be any place."

Of course Gook got tossed in the brig and he stayed there until we got on board ship. He was only a private so there was no way they could punish him by busting him down a rank. But, somehow, he got his hands on a set of clippers on the ship and went back to his trade.

But back to the briefing in the hold of the transport Harris. On the deck inside the hold was a huge painted mock-up of an island that looked something like a lizard with a long tail. In total, we learned it was 1-1/2 miles long and a half mile wide at its widest part. The island was surrounded by a ring of white space marked "coral reef." There were lines drawn on the shore and areas marked "Red Beach 1, Red Beach 2, Red Beach 3 and Green Beach 1."

"This is an island called 'Betio,' " explained a sweaty second lieutenant who had a long wooden pointer in his hand. "Betio is part of the Tarawa Atoll, a string of islands in the mid-Pacific linked by a coral reef. It's got an airfield we want and…uh…and…hey! Wake up that corporal back there!" Corporal Eddie Springmeyer, sitting next to me, had dozed off in the stuffy heat. I gave him a poke. He sat up and rubbed his eyes.

"Don't you think you better pay attention to how this landing is going to come off?" the lieutenant yelled at Springmeyer.

"It won't happen like that, sir." Eddie said. "It never does."

This sparked a roar of laughter from the assembled Marines but it made the lieutenant livid. "Sound off like that again and you go on report!" he yelled at Eddie who drew a long sigh and tried to focus on the Betio Island mockup.

We all quieted down while the lieutenant used the pointer stick to explain what he assured us was going to occur. The bad news was that our unit might not be going in on D-Day with the initial assault battalions. We were attached to the Sixth Infantry Regiment, which was being held in reserve. If we were needed and went in, it would be on Green Beach One. The initial assault, a frontal attack by the Second and Eighth regiments would be hitting Red Beaches One, Two and Three. We were told they would be going in parallel to a long, wooden pier which jutted out into the ocean 400 yards, extending across the rim of shallow coral to deep water. The pier was used by the Japanese for unloading ships and would be needed by our forces after the battle; thus it would not be bombed in the week leading up to the assault. From aircraft carriers and from cruisers and battleships, the island would be pounded by bombs and raked with naval shells, the lieutenant stated.

"This will be the easiest landing you guys will ever make," the lieutenant announced with confidence. "There will be one bomb or one naval shell hit every square yard of the island and nothing could possibly live through it. You will be able to march in at right shoulder arms!"

He also had some aerial photos of the island, which showed a few eight-inch and five-inch gun emplacements, some trenches and a lot of coconut log buildings with thatched roofs. It didn't look like much.

"What are we taking this island for?" someone asked.

The lieutenant wiped the sweat off his face. "We are starting our drive across the central Pacific toward the Island of Japan," he said. "This is the first move and we expect the Japanese Navy to come out and challenge us. That's what our Navy wants. They want to get the Jap Navy out in the open so they can finish it off."

"You mean, we're bait?" the Marine continued.

"Something like that."

To shield our butts from an enemy air assault on the landing, Navy and Army planes would be bombing and strafing all of the known Jap airfields within a day's range of Betio. This was a reassuring piece of information because the last thing we needed was to have the Jap Air Force catch us like sitting ducks in a troop ship. We well remembered the havoc Jap ships and planes created during our invasion of Guadalcanal.

We were dismissed by the lieutenant and filed back up on deck feeling pretty good about the whole thing. "Boy, how about that?" somebody commented. "We can march in tomorrow with our rifles on our shoulders."

Springmeyer gave him a sour look and shook his head. "Don't bet on it."

At daybreak, Nov. 20, we were on deck to watch the show. For a week prior, Navy bombers had been hitting the island, but this morning, D-Day, it was the big guns of the task force firing salvo after salvo at the island. The gunfire was deafening and the island was all but obscured by fire, smoke, flying sand, coral and pieces of coconut trees. On the deck of the Harris, we were looking directly at Green Beach 1, our landing site. From what we could see, it appeared that the lieutenant at the briefing had been right. It didn't look like anything could live through that pounding.

Higgins boats and amphibious tractors were loaded, circled, formed into waves and headed for the beach, each craft leaving a wake of white foam in the blue water. Since we were in reserve, all we could do was watch in envy as the assault teams churned in. Just as the first wave approached the beach, the Navy quit firing and there were a few moments of eerie quiet. Then, as the men of the Eighth and Second Regiments closing in on the island said later: "Everything went to hell in a handbasket."

First, the tide was out and a lot of what we could see looked like mass confusion as boats began to offload their troops a long way from the beach. Suddenly, landing craft began exploding and burning. Troops in the water up to their butts, trying to wade in, were being laced with machine gun fire. Amphib tractors were taking hits although some made it to the beach, disgorging Marines who jammed up behind the coconut log breakwater. Another thing became quickly apparent: When Naval shells hit the log buildings, the logs were blown away exposing concrete blockhouses, some with walls four feet thick. Furthermore, these were designed so they could fire in support of each other and were connected with underground tunnels so the defenders could move back and forth unseen.

From the deck of our ship we picked up fragments of radio messages, terse reports from Marines lucky enough to get to the shore. Surviving amphibs from the first wave were now churning back toward the fleet, supposedly to pick up more troops. Two of the armored tractors veered off toward the Harris, which surprised us because we didn't think were we slated to go in just yet. The reason they came to our troopship became apparent when they pulled up alongside. Both amtraks were jammed with smashed and bloody Marines. The Second Division Hospital Ship was already filled and watercraft with wounded were being directed to any other boats with medical personnel aboard. Crewmen from the Harris immediately lowered wire stretchers to bring up the bloody men. The first couple who were swung over the railing, glared at us in their pain and muttered: "Right shoulder arms, Mac!" in reference to the predictions of an unopposed landing we heard the day before.

From the wounded and from sporadic radio messages, we pieced together a horrific picture of what was occurring between the reef and the shore. It was a fragmented picture because most of the radios weren't working and communications were chaotic. Some units made it to shore with most of their personnel intact, but some were decimated in the water or in the crossfire on the beach. Some Marines hit the shore running and simply by-passed a lot of the concrete bunkers and had gotten somewhere into the island unknown to other units. While casualties were high, they weren't as bad as originally feared because so many units simply had no communications.

The long pier jutting out into the ocean, the one which had been carefully preserved from bombs so we could use later, turned out to be honeycombed with machine gun nests which caught the invading Marines in a terrible flanking fire. Other Marines waded waist deep along the edge of the pier, hunting the gun ports and hurling grenades inside to silence the Jap gunners.

We watched all this carnage in the distance, frustrated that our comrades were getting shot up and we could do nothing to help them. Finally word came down that the troops in reserve were going in. We gathered our gear, ready to board the landing craft. That turned out to be a false alarm mainly because most of the landing craft were immobilized out on the reef or reduced to burned out hulks on the beach. One artillery unit, the First Battalion 10th, went ashore with their guns. Fragmented radio messages indicated that they rolled their 75mm cannons over the seawall, had dug them in like machine guns and were bore sighting them, firing shells point blank at the Jap pill boxes.

Day began to wane and we still weren't committed to the fight. We smoked cigarettes, went below decks and got a few cups of coffee, came back to the rails, stared at the island and swore a lot. Our rifles and packs were piled on the deck waiting for the trip in. Then the sun dipped below the horizon and the tropical night came on swiftly. Still we could see the flashes, the fire, smoke and strings of tracers curving into the darkness. We were right next door to one heck of a battle and we couldn't get our teeth into it.

"Going in at daybreak," the word was passed around. We didn't sleep. We sat on deck and stared at the glowing fires and explosions ashore. Dawn finally came and with it the assurance that our comrades had held their beachhead all night. A few reinforcements had gotten in and one heck of a fight was still in progress.

"Here they come!" A cry went up when a line of landing craft headed for the Harris. Our taxi service was coming at last. Hurriedly, we shouldered our packs and rifles, went over the rail and clambered down the swaying cargo nets into the boats and amphib tractors. Our 75mm guns, dismantled for handling, were lowered in pieces. At last we pulled away from the Harris, circled, formed into a flotilla and began our trip. Only instead of heading straight for the beach, we were traveling parallel to it. Apparently, during the night, division command determined that one more artillery unit cluttering up the beach on Tarawa would simply add to the confusion. Our mission had been changed to land on Bairiki, the next island in the chain. Also, small units of Jap troops had been seen slipping across the reef at low tide, heading for the other islands in the atoll. Our job was to be twofold: We would cut off their escape and also set up to fire on Betio. Instead of landing on a shell-raked beach, we landed unopposed next door on a quiet, palm shaded sand strip that looked like a scene out of a Hollywood tropical movie.

In minutes we had our guns set up, contact established with observers in the melee on Betio and began pumping shells across the small strip of flooded reef into the concrete blockhouses beyond. It was a fire method we had practiced in New Zealand, where observers were on the opposite side of the enemy from the guns, directing fire toward themselves. Periodically, as targets were identified, our guns roared and dozens of shells went howling toward the smoking island.

Just before sunset, Gunnery Sergeant Michalski came over to my foxhole. "Cary, we've got a mission."

"Yeah?"

"We are assigned to take a radio and hike across the reef after dark as soon as the tide goes out and set up an observation post on the tip of Betio behind Jap lines so we can direct more accurate fire."

"You and me?"

"Yeah, two of us. Be ready at dark."

"Roger!"

This was a little more like it. At least Michalski and I would be where the fight was going on although we would be on the Japanese side of the island rather than our own. Still, it started the adrenalin pumping. I could see the rest of the squad was green with envy.

Darkness came and I got my gear together, checked my ammo and grenades, re-checked the radio to make sure it was functioning. Somewhere toward midnight, observers picked out the shadows of several Japs creeping across the reef from Betio. Shots were exchanged and then some grenades went off. The Japs, realizing they were cut off, blew themselves up. But the mission assigned Michalski and I got scrubbed. Somebody up the chain of command decided they didn't want to risk us out on the reef if Japs were coming across. Michalski was madder than a stepped-on rattlesnake and so was I. The night evolved into dawn and with it, the final mop-up occurred directly across the reef from where we were dug in. It had been 36 furious hours of fierce fighting for the men who made it ashore on Tarawa. We had over one-third of the division - nearly 7,000 men - killed or wounded. The Japs had lost over 5,000. All except a very few were dead.

It was an expensive scramble for a mission, which was supposed to be nearly unopposed.

Chapter 10
Tarawa Aftermath

The tide was out. The coral strip between Bairiki and Betio lay glistening white and bare. There was no longer the thump of shells, the stutter of machine guns. All combat activity had ceased. Eddie Springmeyer was sitting on the edge his fox hole drinking milk from a green coconut. "Hey, you wanna take a hike over and see what it looks like?"

"Why the heck not?" We slung our rifles and headed across the glistening white coral reef to the still smoldering ruins of Betio. Before we reached the shore, we could smell death. The 5,000 dead defenders, mostly underground in concrete redoubts, had been cooking in the heat for two or three days. The stench was overpowering.

There were no whole coconut trees left standing on the entire island, only some torn tree trunks and stubs of trees. Churned up sand, steel posts, sand bags, strands of barbed wire, rifles with broken stocks, machine gun belts, and ammo boxes were jumbled together in a disorganized mess. Some shell-scarred concrete bunkers stood out in bleak whiteness. Sandbagged entries to underground tunnels emitted a choking odor. Here and there, a few, dirty, hollow-eyed combat Marines sat on logs or chunks of concrete, smoked cigarettes, ate rations or simply leaned back on their elbows eyeing us without emotion.

Eddie and I picked our way around the rubble, viewed the wrecked five-inch and eight-inch Jap artillery pieces which had so recently wrought havoc with our landing craft and noted a couple of wrecked Marine halftracks, their 75 mm guns pointed toward the sky. Shore units and Graves Registration had carefully picked up all the dead Marines from the water and the beach and had trucked them to a cemetery being created on the coral sand. Bulldozers were digging trenches and shoveling in whatever dead Japanese could be found above ground. The litter of war lay everywhere- Jap rifles, uniforms, machine guns, metal clips, unused grenades, shoes, helmets, bayonets, artillery shells and shell casings. Some of the live stuff looked like it might go off with a good kick. We avoided it.

"The tide is coming in," Eddie noted at length. "We better head back or we will be swimming back." We had seen enough and smelled enough of the residue of war. We hiked back across the reef as the water began slopping against our shoes. After war-torn Betio, the shady palm beaches and fresh air of Bairiki were a relief. Shirtless Marines in work details were unloading supplies from Higgins boats. Some men, off duty, lounged beneath the palms. A handful of native islanders and a white man in missionary garb arrived from other islands and stopped to talk. They said a platoon of Japanese soldiers had passed through the islands a couple of days earlier and were no doubt still out there somewhere. We told them a company from the Sixth Regiment was combing the islands, seeking the missing Japs.

"Guess what tomorrow is?" somebody said. "Thanksgiving!"

96

The living had a lot to be thankful for. Most of us wrote letters home letting our families know we had escaped the carnage of Betio. We knew they would be reading about the heavy casualties of the Second Marine Division, about the veterans of Guadalcanal who had been cut down on the beaches in a swift, bloody assault. We wanted to quickly assure our folks that we were not among the casualties. And we knew, sadly, that several thousand letters would be going out to other families starting off: "The United States Marine Corps regrets to inform you..."

But those of us alive had time to light fires, heat water, wash laundry, get shaved and cleaned up. On the horizon, where blue sky met a blue Pacific Ocean, cruisers and battleships were riding at anchor. Small boats were bringing in a steady stream of supplies to the long pier which only days before had shielded the Jap machine guns that exacted such a terrible toll.

"Work detail!" Gunnery Sergeant Hogue called out. He rounded up about 20 of us and we followed him to the shore where Higgins boats were bringing in a steady stream of 75 and 105mm artillery shells. "Hey, Gunny," Somebody asked. "The battle is over. Why the heck are we unloading these shells?"

"Navy probably doesn't want to sail all around the ocean with a load of live ammo," Hogue guessed.

A Navy shore party had already started two stacks, piling High Explosives in one pile marked "H.E." and Armor Piercing in another, smaller pile, with a sign reading "A.P." The temperature in the sun was over 100 degrees and burning hot by any standard. The shells were in cloverleaves of threes, 50 to 75 pounds each of heavy lifting. We unloaded, hauled and sweated until we had completed two mountains of shells on the sand. A supply captain came down the beach to check this over, stopped short and stared. "For cripes sake!" he bawled. "You guys got the stacks reversed. You've got high explosive and the armor piercing in the wrong piles!"

We stopped for a moment and stared at our work. Sure

enough. We had stacked the Armor Piercing by the sign reading "H.E." and the High Explosive by the sign reading "A.P."

The captain swore about dumb jarheads. Hogue swore about the dumb Navy work party that started the stacks in the first place. With considerable grumbling, we all got busy moving the High Explosive and the Armor Piercing to the right piles. An hour later, we had just gotten finished when Hogue let out a snort and swore some more.

"What's the matter now, Gunny?" somebody asked.

"Migod, we moved all that ammo," Hogue observed. "All we had to do was move the two signs."

Sometimes in the military you get so busy obeying orders, you never stop to think what you are doing.

* * * * * * * *

Squads of combat Marines were being taxied by Higgins boat from Betio to board transports, to get them away from the stink and wreckage as quickly as possible. But on Bairiki, life was much easier. A few Marines played poker on ponchos and some read tattered paperback books. For those of us who had escaped the fray, there was a sense of how lucky we were but also the frustration of trained warriors who had been denied their war. Evening came with a blazing sunset, gently murmuring surf and the sound of seagulls on arched wings crying shrilly over the reef. The setting was like a tropical movie only there was no background orchestra and no scantily-clad Hollywood starlets swaying on the beach.

At sunrise, we were awakened by shouts from a handful of Marines wading out on the reef. Heart-shaped native fish traps, about 75 feet in diameter with walls of coral blocks, were full of thrashing fish. They were mostly three-foot, silvery mackerel which had moved over the reef in huge schools when the tide was in, bumped into the traps and swam along until they hit the "throat" where there was an opening in the rock wall. They swam into the traps and were stranded there when the tide went out. A dozen Marines were wading about in the fish traps, grabbing big mackerel by their tails and carrying them to shore. In minutes, most of Fox Battery was out on the reef, wading among the thrashing fish and then coming out, each of us with a four-to-six-pound mackerel in each hand.

The harvest was not without hazard. Some of the first Marines had taken off their boots and waded out barefoot, a maneuver that resulted in slashed feet from the sharp coral. We quickly found that we had to keep our shoes on or risk serious injury. Also, we had to pay attention to where we placed our feet. A few unwary Marines stepped on moray eels and received severe leg bites.

The mackerel were broad, fat, bright silver fish with tails shaped like half moons. We carried them to shore by dozens, dressed them, built fires and baked them over the coals. Some accommodating natives shinnied up palm trees and knocked down green coconuts filled with cool milk. Our 1943 Thanksgiving dinner consisted of a feast of freshly baked fish and coconut milk. We gorged on our catch and then stretched out in the shade to smoke, talk about life back home and what we would be doing when the war was over. More transports appeared on the horizon, ships which would take us to our new base in Hawaii, there to be re-equipped and the mass of casualties replaced. But a lot more war was left to be fought. Much more.

We were aware our division officer corps had taken a beating and there would be re-shuffling of command and some new faces. Many enlisted personnel were transferred to other units that had sustained heavy casualties. Along with a number of comrades with whom I had served, even gone though basic training in San Diego, I received orders assigning me to Headquarters and Service Company in the same battalion. We hated like the dickens to leave our old buddies at Fox Battery, but we knew the moves were necessary. We were battle-tested and confident we could handle any job assigned. We were like members of a well-trained football team with an unbeaten record. We were good at what we did and we knew we were the point men of the American spearhead aimed at the heart of the Japanese Empire.

Other troops were striking the Marshall Islands. To the west, MacArthur's men were mopping up in New Guinea and getting ready to retake the Philippines. In Europe, General Eisenhower was laying the plans for the invasion of France. It had been a long haul from Pearl Harbor, but for us the picture was beginning to take shape. We did not know the big moves behind the scenes. We did not know about the nuclear bombs being developed at Los Alamos and certainly not that the Germans had been on the track of the same weapons, their time table thrown off by a team of Norwegian commandos who blew up one of Hitler's critical facilities in Norway. We only knew that we had some tough training ahead, more islands to invade, more enemy to defeat.

Higgins boats eventually picked us up with our pea-shooter 75mm cannons and hauled us out to the transports in the bay. With rifles and full packs, we went up the cargo nets to the steel decks above, were assigned bunks in the steamy hold, stowed our gear and lined up for supper, a real supper, at the ship's mess. Word was we were heading for Hawaii, the Paradise Islands of song and story. And for once the scuttlebutt was fairly accurate. Zigzagging for submarine evasion, the flotilla of ships plowed north and east toward the islands where the Japanese had first struck on Dec. 7, 1941. First stop: Honolulu on the island of Oahu.

Hoo, boy! From movies we anticipated bamboo huts with thatched roofs and brown skinned young ladies undulating in grass skirts to the throbbing of drums and seductive tropical music. From the rail of the transport, we stared as we came into dock. We could see some sand beaches and palm trees. But the bamboo huts had been replaced by brick and chrome offices and high rises. The ramp went down and most of us were allowed to go ashore. Downtown Honolulu was a mass of humanity and bustling traffic. It was like any other big city except the people were mostly smaller, browner and looked a lot more like the people we had recently been fighting. And they didn't pay us one bit of attention. People in uniform were no novelty in Honolulu.

Since none of us had any money, there was not much we could do except walk around. Carl Houston, Earl Englehardt and I wandered down to the former Royal Palace near Waikiki Beach, then walked to the beach itself. Here we removed our shoes and sox and went wading in the surf, allowing that we could at least write home that we had gone wading at Waikiki Beach.

Then it was back to the ship. Our next stop was Hilo on the big island of Hawaii. Trucks awaited to transport us to our new base - a bunch of tents in a desolate stretch of treeless real estate at the foot of Mauna Kea, one of the more active volcanoes on the island. It was one that incessantly smoked and sputtered; threatening to erupt and finish off whatever part of the Division the Japs had missed on Tarawa.

There was a lot of loud complaining as we unloaded the trucks and moved into our tents. First Sergeant Bittick, tired of the grousing, let out a bellow: "This is the Marine Corps! What the hell did you expect, the Waldorf Astoria?"

What indeed? It was time to think about our next invasion.

Chapter 11
Foraging

In the parlance of military language, it's called "foraging." That is, if the troops are in need, it is acceptable, perhaps even advisable, to venture into the surrounding countryside for whatever is required. History tells us that in the Civil War, both Union and Confederate forces relied to a considerable extent on foraging to survive. In Marine parlance it means "scrounge something up." Usually, this involves food, such as seeking out farm produce, livestock, poultry, whatever, but not always. Not in that particular instance involving Fox Battery in Hawaii.

The Second Division came to Hawaii in the aftermath of Tarawa. Landing on the big island at the port city of Hilo we were trucked to a barren site between Mauna Kea, and Mauna Loa, two far-from-extinct volcanoes that hissed and sputtered nightly and threatened to blow themselves up and us along with them. Two evenings we experienced earthquakes, probably not massive on the Richter Scale, but enough to make the ground shake and the tents sway. There was comment that what the Japanese forces failed to do on Tarawa, the mountains might.

We always held a belief that the Marine Corps central command nurtured teams of sadistic advance personnel whose sole purpose was to find the most uninhabitable places on earth upon which to locate Second Division camps. This site, 65 miles inland, was located on black volcano dust that turned into black muck whenever it rained. Since we arrived there in winter, it rained a lot and there was plenty of muck.

The nearest village was Kamuela, a scanty collection of frame houses, a bar, a store, a gas station and not much else. A little farther away was the village of Honakaa, not much of a recreational improvement. Our immediate concern, however, was to create livable quarters on the barren camp site, erect mess halls, storage buildings and offices and lay out rows of wooden tent platforms upon which rested rows of six-man canvas tents. Food, much better than K rations, was adequate. Cots and blankets eventually showed up to shield us from the December cold and we even had a movie theater under construction. Why, then, was there a need for foraging? Simply because the Second Division had no shoes.

The hard, sharp coral, which lay under Tarawa atoll, had shredded the bottoms of our shoes. Hardly anyone had a pair of shoes without holes in the soles. We had sore feet, cut feet, and soggy feet from rain and muck that oozed up through the holes. Finally, word came down that a half-mile-long supply train had pulled into the siding at Kamuela. We all anticipated new shoes. And there were no complaints when Fox Battery received orders to send a detail down to help unload the boxcars. My squad drew the midnight-to-four a.m. shift and we arrived to find floodlights illuminating the rail siding, MP's all over the place and a long line of idling trucks in a fog of exhaust, waiting to be loaded.

Dismay began to creep in when we realized we would be unloading beer. Hundreds upon hundreds of cases. Ordinarily, this would have been a welcome activity since it was relatively easy to drop a case and have the cardboard carton break open on one side. A broken case was considered damaged goods, which could be set aside, out of the way, while the intact ones were moved. An occasional bottle could be spirited out of the broken case for immediate use. But beer we did not need. Not at that point when our feet were killing us. We guessed that somewhere in that long line of freight cars there was replacement clothing and shoes. But when would that get unloaded and supplied to the troops?

As we limped across the gravel in the glare of the flood-lights, carrying unending cases of beer to the waiting trucks, the term "forage" came to mind. Within my squad was a PFC named Nolte who claimed to come from a railroad family and who had worked in a railyard prior to enlisting. I signaled him to one side of the boxcar and pointed out that somewhere in this long line of rail cars there must be several loaded with shoes.

"Do you know how to open a locked box car?" I asked.

"Yeah."

"OK. You go around behind the line of cars - on the dark side away from the floodlights and MP's - and search for a car with shoes. If you find one, hustle back and we'll figure something out." He nodded, slipped out of the boxcar full of beer and vanished into the night.

In the meantime, we were busy packing case after case of beer to the waiting trucks under the watchful eyes of the MP's. Their concern was that nobody swiped a case or two. There were 15 of us in the detail, so the MP's never noticed Nolte being gone. A half hour went by and Nolte slipped back into the beer car. "I found the shoes," he whispered. "About 20 cars down."

"Fine. Hold on while I check out our truckers."

At this point I eased out of the boxcar, calmly lit a cigarette in front of the MP's and sauntered over to the line of trucks. As each truck was loaded with beer, it pulled out of the floodlit area and headed off into the darkness to the division supply dump where another set of guards supervised the unloading, Every few minutes a truck was loaded, left and the line moved up.

"Listen," I confided to our lead truck driver, who was about four vehicles from the front of the line. "When you get your next truckload of beer, head for the dump as quick as possible. Then double time back and drive down the opposite side of the train with your lights off, away from the floodlights. There's a gravel road parallel to the tracks. I'll be out there to signal with a flashlight. Pull up where you see us."

"What are we getting, Sarge?" the driver asked.

"Shoes, for cripes sake. We've located a freight car of shoes. We'll load you up, you turn around double time back to the company tent area, unload, then double time back here to get in line for a our next load of beer."

"What if we get caught? Why don't we just keep going until the quartermaster gets to the shoes and then wait for division to issue them?" the trucker asked.

"For one thing, it will take days to unload all this beer. The other thing, even if the shoes get to the division supply dump, there is no telling when the shoes will get to us."

"Yeah, you're right. See you in a half hour." He drove his truck into the floodlit area, we loaded it up with beer and he vanished into the night. The detail kept moving beer cases while Nolte and I and two others slipped around to the dark side of the train and made our way down to where the box car with the shoes was waiting.

It seemed like an hour, but it was less than 20 minutes when our truck came back, easing down the gravel roadway in the dark, lights turned off. I signaled with the flashlight and the truck driver eventually pulled up and stopped. Nolte had the box car door wide open and we went to work with the flashlight, picking out cartons of shoes in a variety of sizes. It took only 15 minutes to load up the truck. Nolte secured the box car door. The truck driver turned around and headed back toward our camp. Nobody in the floodlit area on the other side of the train had any idea what was happening on the dark side. We returned to the lighted side and kept unloading beer until 4 a.m., when we were relieved.

Back in the company area, we had a mountain of cardboard cartons with over 200 pairs of shoes stacked outside First Sergeant Bittick's tent. I stuck my head inside and aimed my flashlight at his face. He was sound asleep, snoring up a storm.

"Bittick!" I hissed.

His eyes flickered open and he blinked in the light. "Get that thing out of my face. Whatta you want?"

"It's me, Cary. We've got a truckload of shoes out on the company street."

Bittick glanced at his watch. "For cripes sakes, it is only 4:30. Wake me up when it's daylight."

"No. The shoes are hot. We stole 'em off the train."

"Oh migod!" Bittick jerked upright in his cot, swung his legs over the side and began pulling on his pants. "We got to get rid of them."

"Right."

Bittick snapped on his own flashlight and followed me out to the company street. When he saw the pile of shoe cartons, he let out a whistle "Oh migod! Listen, go around and get everybody up. We've got to have a clothing requisition right now, quick, and get rid of these boxes."

Inside of 10 minutes we had the whole company out in the street, most of them in their underwear, including the officers. Bittick detailed several noncoms to hand out shoes to the men in whatever sizes were needed. For about 45 minutes there was a furious clothing issue in the night.

"What size?"

"Ten E."

"Here you are, move out!

By daybreak, everyone had new shoes. All the cardboard cartons had been stamped flat and stuck in the division garbage dump behind the mess hall. When we fell out for roll call, everyone had a grin on his face, including the captain. Nobody was limping because of holes in his shoes.

The only thing was, when we had our next battalion formation, Fox Battery was the only unit with new shoes, a circumstance not lost on the Battalion Commander. He called the captain out of ranks and wanted to know where the shoes came from. The captain, straight faced, said the first sergeant had reported that each Marine had an extra pair in his sea bag before we went to Tarawa. That was kind of true because the First Sergeant really told the captain to say it. The colonel didn't buy that for a minute but there was no evidence that we had pulled off some kind of a heist. A least not for two more days until the train pulled forward and the work crews came upon the somewhat depleted box car of shoes. However, Nolte had jumbled the remaining boxes to make it appear that maybe that particular boxcar hadn't been loaded full. Anyway, Division Supply was holding daily requisitions of clothing and gear so the matter simply vanished.

Well, not entirely. Even though everyone in the regiment now had new shoes, the colonel still looked at Fox Company with considerable suspicion. Bittick braced me one day on the parade ground. "Listen, you gonna pull off something like that again, you talk to me first."

"I'll keep that in mind," I said. After all, it was a little late for discussion.

Chapter 12
Vacation Time

It was the unfairness of it all. That's how we got in trouble, Houston, Englehardt and me. Maybe the award ceremony helped. That was not exactly a great cause for celebration.

Because the division had taken a severe beating on Tarawa, the worst in Marine Corps history, and even though the operation was a necessity and we won, the Japanese had inflicted some very serious damage on the Second Division. It was a heck of a 76-hour fight and the men who won it earned every plaudit the nation could bestow. Still, the Division took a shellacking and in most such cases, the high command and the political establishment make every attempt to put on a good face. In our case, President Roosevelt awarded the Presidential Unit Citation to the Second Division.

To receive the award, what was left of Second Division was trucked 50 miles to the high school football field in the City of Hilo and assembled in ranks before a large review stand decorated with red, white and blue bunting. Those of us who were at Tarawa knew who took the brunt of the assault. Those of us in The Second Battalion, 10th Marines, knew we played a near-negligible part. We had landed on the adjacent island of Bairiki to block the Japs from retreat and to form another invasion point on the east end of the main island of Betio, if necessary. The Second, Sixth and Eighth Regiments had gotten hammered along with the First Battalion, 10th. Basically, the award ceremony was their show.

As was usual, we were assembled on the football field a long time before anything was about to happen. Hurry up and wait. It was a pleasant day, warm and clear...but boring. We formed ranks, snapped to attention and then stood at parade rest. When there was nothing else to do, we came to attention again and back to parade rest. In the middle of all this make-busy, six large mongrel dogs came bouncing out of a nearby bunch of houses and proceeded to hold their own inspection. They ran up and down the rows of troops, enjoying getting their heads petted and muzzles scratched. This minor disruption generated considerable disapproval among some of the more rank-conscious officers who called their units to attention and tried to get the dogs shooed off the field, without success.

Eventually, the high brass appeared in black limos decorated with tiny American flags. They stopped at the edge of the football field and their occupants disembarked. We strained our eyes to make out the figures. From where we were, they looked like the photos we had seen of Secretary of the Navy Frank Knox, Admiral Bull Halsey, Admiral Chester Nimitz, General Julian Smith, Colonel Merritt Edson and a few others we couldn't identify. As they marched single file to the steps of the reviewing stand, we were again called to attention, this time in rigid appreciation of the importance of the occasion. The band struck up a lively march.

At that point, the six dogs left the assembled Marines and

headed for the reviewing stand. Four of those dogs were males and as they filed past, each lifted his right rear leg and urinated on the red, white and blue stage. First a terse giggle went up from the ranks and then a throaty roar of laughter swept the assembly. This promptly brought gruff orders to "Shut Up! Knock It Off! Act like Marines!" But the damage was done. Perhaps the dogs broke the tense feeling of resentment for the thousands of comrades we lost, many we felt to bad planning and poor preparation. The laughter waned, then broke out all over again. From the rear ranks somebody shouted: "Give the dogs a medal!"

Some speeches were made by the assembled dignitaries, but the only thing we could remember later was what the dogs did to the reviewing stand. Eventually the program ended, we were bundled back in the trucks and deposited at Camp Tarawa, which is where Houston, Englehardt and I hatched our plan for a furlough.

See, an order had come down as soon as we landed in Hawaii, that everyone still healthy and mobile in the Second Division was entitled to 10 days leave. This was to be done in three stages. Houston, Englehardt and I were squad leaders and our concern was for the men under us. Thus we assigned the first 10 days of leave to the bottom ranks - privates and PFC's. We determined that the corporals would be next and then the sergeants - us. The trouble was, dozens of replacements were coming in, lots of construction was underway and Division Command was in a sweat to get the camp operational and new men trained. Thus the second echelon of leave was scaled back to five days. Still, that was reasonable. But before the corporals finished their vacations, all leaves were cancelled. And that, we felt, was totally unfair.

Houston, Englehardt and I quietly discussed this at some length over coffee in the NCO mess and determined to take the vacation we felt we were promised. We each had over $150 back pay on the books and Englehardt had made contact with a taxi driver, the only one in Kamuella, who would drive us over to the resort village of Kona, 50 miles away, for $40, total. We picked Kona because we had heard it was gorgeous and had been the setting for a pre-war Bing Crosby movie titled "Blue Hawaii."

Our next move was to get one-day passes from Butler, the company clerk, who was also the company bugler. We didn't particularly like Butler and he didn't particularly like us, but we offered a bribe of a quart of whiskey if he would fix things up. We not only got the necessary papers for a day in town, but also assurance from the clerk that in the event we were a trifle tardy getting back, he would mark us down as being present for bed check. This required the promise of a second bottle. Of course, Butler had no way of knowing we weren't coming back. At least not right away.

We drew our money off the books and each packed a small bag of toiletries. We contacted the taxi driver and headed for vacationland. There was nothing impressive in the drive across the middle of the big island, but Kona was a gem. It consisted of picturesque thatched roof bistros and lots of atmosphere, right on the shore of incredible, foam-washed surf. Since we were already somewhat illegal, we sought out a less conspicuous hide-out, settling on a white frame rooming house run by a wrinkled Chinese lady who put us up for $1.50 a night, each. It was clean, looked out on the ocean and seemed secure from prying MP's whom, we were sure, would soon be looking for us.

We stayed indoors until sunset then ventured up the main street, eventually arriving at the plush Kona Hotel, where a gala Army-Navy party was in progress. It should have dawned on us that we were totally out of place because there was no one involved in the festivities below the rank of lieutenant. There were Army majors and colonels, Air Force colonels, Army WAAC captains and high-ranking nurses, Navy commanders and even full captains. All high brass. And then we three Marine buck sergeants. The thing was, the officers quickly found out we were fresh from the smoke and blood of Tarawa and they wanted to hear some war stories. So we told war stories. Some dandies. Some were almost true. And they bought endless rounds of refreshments so we didn't run dry. Heck of a night. Eventually, things came to a soggy conclusion and we wandered back to the rooming house about 3 a.m. and holed up the rest of the night and the next day. That night was a repeat of the first: more party, more stories, more fun. And back to the rooming house.

Somewhere during the celebration, Englehardt had picked up a travel folder listing local attractions. Among them was the Little Grass Shack in Kealakekua, an edifice about which a popular song of that era had been written. The folder said that for a couple of bucks, visitors could have their pictures taken in front of the grass shack by a local photographer. Englehardt and Houston insisted we hike up there, a couple of miles off, and have our photos taken to send home. Because of possible police implications, my instincts were not to venture out in daylight, but I was overruled. So off we went.

The grass shack and the photographer were there as advertised. We each had a photo taken, paid for a couple of prints and headed back down the road to Kona. That's when our luck ran out. We almost made it back when a jeep with two Marine MPs on board pulled up and we were placed under arrest.

Unfortunately, while waiting for our prints in Kealakekua, Englehardt had purchased a bottle in a local liquor establishment. I was still feeling the effects from the previous two nights, but my companions set about tapping into their new supply. When the Jeep pulled up with the gendarmes wearing official MP armbands, Houston let out a cry of alarm and said, "Let's run for it!"

Obviously, he was in no condition to run anywhere. He promptly fell headfirst into the roadside ditch where the MP's collared him. Englehardt and I didn't make a move, but we were all busted for "breaking arrest' among other infractions.

We had been smart enough to get an official one-day leave from the company clerk so our offense was Absent Over Leave (AOL), not quite as severe as Absent With Out Leave (AWOL) for which one may be shot in wartime. In any event, we were hauled back to Camp Tarawa under arrest, duly court-martialed, convicted, marched out in front of the battalion and heard the charges read off. In addition to the Absent Over Leave charge, we were charged with being out of bounds (it turned out that Kona was reserved for officers only and no enlisted personnel were allowed there); we were not in full khaki and were charged with being "out of uniform". Englehardt's jug was an illegal possession and since we had tapped it a couple of times, we were booked as "drunk and disorderly." In all, there were 14 separate offenses read off at our court-martial. The last was "conduct unbecoming members of the Marine Corps," one they always listed just in case some of the first ones didn't stick. Nobody mentioned the fact that we had been gypped out of 10 days promised leave, a contributing factor. Our sentences, assigned by the Battalion Commander, were uniform: Fourteen days bread and water in solitary, and six months confinement to camp. We were not busted down in rank, which was not too bad, considering. We dutifully served five days and then, wonder of wonders, we were released to First Sergeant Bittick. Two truckloads of replacements had arrived and all sergeants were needed to train the newcomers in the arts of mayhem and massacre.

Houston, Englehardt and I, of course, were confined to camp as Prisoners At Large (PAL's) and required to report at 8 a.m., noon, 4 p.m. and 9 p.m., daily. And we each wore dungarees with a huge, white "P" stenciled on the back to identify our situation. On our first day with the assembled replacements, one rookie asked, "What does the "P" stand for on your dungarees?"

"Ha!" replied Houston, with dignity. "P is for Perfect! You have to attain the highest enlisted approval rating to get a 'P' on your dungarees!" It was some time before the replacements discovered the truth.

There was only one real drawback to our Kona adventure, outside of having it cut short by the MP's. Butler, the company clerk, who issued our leave papers and signed us in when we weren't there, was nailed for false muster. He was already in confinement when we were arrested. And he didn't get out as quickly as we did. Let us say he was rather bitter about the whole matter.

When the clerk was finally released from the brig and restored to duty, we gave our remaining resources to Sergeant Zembles and had him pick up two quarts of cheap whiskey in Kamuela. Thus we fulfilled our commitment as best we could. We agreed it was only fair that we keep our word. At least that part of it. Butler, however, was furious and stayed furious. Houston thought he lacked a sense of humor.

Chapter 13
How to Get Home

Maybe it was the depressing setting. There are truly parts of Hawaii which are absolutely magnificent. The coast, in particular, is incredible; but where Camp Tarawa was situated, it was 50 points below dismal. If the weather was dry, the volcano dust blew all over and if it rained, the volcano dust turned into goo.

There were few trees anywhere near camp. Towering overhead were two sputtering volcanoes - Mauna Loa and Mauna Kea, both of which threatened to blow up anytime. On occasion, we experienced minor earthquakes which further increased our suspicion that this area was far from stable. Some of our more philosophical brothers at arms opined that the Marine Corps picked such a miserable camp site so that combat would be much more preferable. In any event, most of us stoically toughed it out; but a few really had it up to here with the Marine Corps and determined to take measures.

Sergeant Charlie Doss had a pretty good combat record in Guadalcanal, but after Tarawa he decided he didn't want to be a Marine any more. Especially at Camp Tarawa. We had a few like that along the way - Marines who decided, after the fact that they were in the wrong line of work. We had one on Guadalcanal who decided to get wounded so he could be sent home. The Japanese would gladly oblige if a Marine got careless. It was relatively easy to get shot; but PFC Conlon couldn't wait. Besides, if you got shot by a Jap, you might get killed instead of wounded, a rather depressing thought. So he shot himself in the foot. There was considerable black humor about this kind of thing and there were probably a number of others who did it; but this guy was ridiculous. I think his name was Conlon; but I can't be sure, 60 years later. In any event, it was a quiet day. The regular morning downpour had ended, the temperature was closing in on 100 degrees Fahrenheit, and the jungle was steaming. Mosquitoes were out and there was no indication of a war going on anywhere. And then there was this loud bang. A single rifle shot. One bang on a quiet day is apt to get anyone's attention. The tendency is to duck and determine what caused the shot; but it wasn't a Japanese sniper bang. It was a .30-06 U.S. bang. We were pretty good at identifying sounds of different weapons. This was definitely one of ours. Next, we heard somebody calling for a corpsman, yelling: "I'm hit! I'm hit!!" A few of us hiked over to see what the heck was going on.

PFC Conlon, in obvious pain, was sitting on the edge of his foxhole, gripping his right foot with both hands, blood leaking down his fingers. "I got shot!" he yelled. "Where's the corpsman?"

"How'd you get shot?" someone inquired.

"Sniper!" he squawked.

There was obviously no sniper. There was Conlon sitting on the edge of his foxhole with a hole in his foot and there was his Springfield rifle. A staff sergeant grabbed the rifle, smelled the muzzle, nodded grimly, checked the magazine and ejected one empty brass cartridge case. The corpsman arrived and provided Conlon with first aid. Then the wounded Marine was bundled off to the aid station where the battalion doctor determined that from the powder burns, the wound was self-inflicted. "If Conlon got shot by a sniper," the doctor said, "the sniper was no more than two feet away." Conlon was shipped off to the brig.

But Charlie Doss had a different approach. "I'm going to throw a fit," he announced at the NCO mess.

"Whatta you mean?" Sergeant Wyatt asked.

"I mean, I am going to go nuts and they have to send me home for a medical discharge."

This created considerable laughter. "When you enlisted in the Marine Corps you were already nuts," Sergeant Crosswise observed. "But that won't get you out."

"Yeah, but if I am raving crazy, they've got to give me a Section Eight discharge."

We all knew Section Eight was for mental cases. Serious ones. Most of us never gave it a thought, but apparently Doss did.

"How are you going to convince them you are nuts?" Von Gremp asked.

"When I throw the fit right after supper tomorrow night."

Naturally, this was the main topic of conversation that night and the next day. Half the NCO's thought Doss was kidding. The other half thought he meant it. But the word got around that Charlie Doss was going to pitch a fit after supper and try for a Section Eight. Just about everybody wanted to see how he was going to carry it off. It was never clear how Doss thought he as going to keep his caper secret from the officers when he was blabbing all over the place. Maybe he really was nuts.

Another thing. Charlie was one of the few men in the battalion with a radio which made him fairly popular, since hanging out at his tent you could hear music and what news there was. At least the war news. We could find out what was going on in other parts of the Pacific. There was some conjecture as to who would get the radio if Charlie was sent home. We didn't know the radio was included in Charlie's theatrical enterprise.

After supper, the following night, Charlie went to his tent and got his radio. Then he headed up the company street, between the rows of canvas tents. Mauna Loa was sputtering as usual and made nice backdrop for the show. As Charlie walked up the street into the officer's area he began uttering some growls and shrieks. He had a pretty good audience since just about all the enlisted men knew his plan. Charlie got louder and louder but none of the officers appeared. Finally, he stopped outside of the doctor's tent and emitted a few blood-curdling yells. Nothing happened. Next, he began raving, threw the radio on the ground and began jumping up and down on it, reducing it to rubble. Still, there was no indication the doctor or any of the officers were interested.

Next, Charlie pulled aside the flap on the doctor's tent and stormed inside yelling. At that point, things grew suddenly quiet. Then we heard what sounded like a dog barking and some shuffling around. Then Charlie emerged from the doctor's tent looking somewhat subdued.

"How'd it go?" someone asked.

Charlie shook his head. "I went into the doc's tent, dropped down on my hands and knees and began barking at him, "Charlie said.

"What happened?"

"The doctor got down on his hands and knees and barked back. Then he shoved his face up to mine and said: "Kid, I can't go home until this crummy war is over and you sure as hell aren't going home, either."

Charlie stared sadly at the pulverized remains of his radio, shrugged and shuffled dejectedly back to his tent. Eventually, he did get sent home, but it was sometime later with malaria, not a mental disorder. At least, not a diagnosed one.

We actually did have one case of someone going home, but without any wounds, sickness or even wanting to go. Corporal Eddie Haley and Corporal George Willis were buddies. They came from the same home town in California, had enlisted together, wound up in Fox Battery together and went through Guadalcanal together. And both contracted malaria. The Division command had set up a quota for a set number of malaria victims to be shipped back to the States as replacements became available. Haley got lucky and received orders to ship stateside. We all knew this and bid him Godspeed and good luck. A couple of guys who lived near his home town asked if he would look up their families and say hello for them. He wrote down the names and addresses and promised to do this. It was on a Sunday that he shouldered his sea bag and was hauled to town in a truck with three others from the battalion. Willis got a one-day pass to town and went with Haley to see him off.

We heard what happened from some other Marines who were at the dock in Wellington. All the Marines going home, Haley included, were in line to go up the gangway onto the troopship. Willis was walking along with his buddy, talking and having a cigarette. When Haley got to the gangway, Willis said so long and stepped to one side. A Marine guard yelled at him: "Hey, you! Get back in line!"

Willis protested that he wasn't supposed to go, but the guard got irate: "Listen! I said get the hell back in line, buddy, or I'll crack your head with this rifle butt."

Willis quickly stepped in line behind Haley and they both went up the gangway onto the ship. Of course, Willis didn't come back from Wellington and the First Sergeant began asking around if anyone had seen him. Somebody had witnessed the whole event and filled in the First Sergeant. He couldn't believe it, but division radio contact was established with the ship, now on its way to San Francisco. Yeah, they had a Corporal Willis on board with no papers. Yeah, he was locked up in the ship's brig and would stay there until the ship got to the states, at which point he would be transferred to another ship heading back to New Zealand.

It was several weeks later when Corporal Willis came back. We had a nice "welcome home" reception for him at the NCO mess and over a couple cases of beer got all the details of his adventure first hand.

"I got a boat ride from New Zealand to San Francisco, but I was in the brig so I couldn't even see the ocean. They transferred me to the brig on another ship coming this way, so I came back and still never got to see the ocean or the Golden Gate Bridge, either. It was a lousy trip. All I did was read magazines and sleep."

Everybody in the NCO mess thought the whole episode was hilarious. And the Division brass couldn't do anything to Willis because it was clear he tried to keep from going on the ship in the first place. But we agreed with him it was crummy that they didn't allow him at least one night on the town when the ship docked at San Francisco. Obviously, nobody at the division level had much of a sense of humor.

Chapter 14
Doing MP Duty

Her nickname was Tondeleyo, a tall black-haired Hawaiian woman of pleasant demeanor who tended a bar in Honakaa, at one of two oases catering to thirsty Marines in the nearby small town. Carl Houston and I were on duty at Tondeleyo's place on a warm Saturday night, lounging against the back wall and making sure the customers in uniform were not becoming unruly. As sergeants, Carl and I pulled MP duty every three weeks, a rather disagreeable task since it usually involved a lot of disorderly young men, some of whom we knew. When some overindulging Jarhead had obviously passed his limit, we caught the bartender's eye, pointed a nightstick and shook our heads. The boisterous trooper found his booze promptly shut off. In most cases, he would yell for more, and receiving none, stalk out of Tondeleyo's club uttering foul invective.

Upon occasion, the subject of our attention became abusive and attempted to climb over the bar to reach the bottled

123

goods on the shelf behind. At this point we stepped forward, smacked the recalcitrant Marine smartly on his buttocks with a night stick and secured him in an arm lock as he came back to his point of origin. Then one, or both of us, ushered him out to a line of waiting trucks manned by other MP's. When a truck was full, it returned to camp, dumped its load of celebrants and returned for more.

Most of the Marines who visited Honakaa on a Saturday night, would quietly stow a few beers, perhaps take in a film at the lone movie theater and hook a ride back to camp. They caused no trouble and received none. But there were a few who thought they were John Wayne in a wild west saloon and wanted to let off some steam with fisticuffs, boots or whatever furniture was handy. These were the problem children we had to deal with.

Both Carl and I had attended MP school as part of our training. We were fairly adept at various forms of martial arts including karate and judo. Perhaps our most valuable instruction was in the use of nightsticks since these were the only armament we carried. The Division Command was well aware that a very drunk and very belligerent trooper might grab a firearm from the holster of an MP and get somebody shot, thus we packed no firearms. The nightstick was deemed weapon enough.

There are a couple dozen uses for the police nightstick in rendering a violent antagonist less belligerent. None of these involve hitting the culprit over the head. If backed into a defensive situation, where our safety was at risk, we could bring the stick, two-handed, across the assailant's nose or drive the butt of the stick into his solar plexus; but this was only when in dire peril. Mainly, we used the nightstick to block blows and kicks from drunks, to lock onto the wrists of would-be assailants, or in a real confrontation, smash him sharply on the inside of the shin-bone, a move which inevitably resulted in near-paralysis of the offender. We had total confidence in our ability and never went on MP duty with any feeling of apprehension.

On this particular Saturday evening, we had escorted a few unruly patrons from Tondeleyo's emporium when all hell broke loose up the street. As we stepped out on the sidewalk for a look, a fellow MP sergeant by the name of Ed Lauterbach came running up, his shirt torn, one eye swollen half shut, and his MP armband gone along with his nightstick. Lauterbach, it should be noted, had missed MP training, a shortcoming which contributed considerably to his present state.

"We've got a riot up at the Tradewinds!" he yelled, wild-eyed. "We need help immediately!"

The three of us legged it fast up the street to the Tradewinds where Lauterbach's assessment proved totally accurate. About 40 half-drunk Marines were in a massive brawl, breaking beer bottles, rendering tables and chairs into kindling and generally making a wreck of the place.

"Maybe we need more MPs!" Lauterbach suggested.

"Probably not, Eddie," growled Carl, starting for a cluster of combatants fighting furiously in the entryway. I piled in behind him. Moving swiftly into the crowd, bent over at the waist, we swung our nightsticks with all force possible against every shinbone within reach. One solid smack on the inside of the shin sent a shock of paralyzing pain through each rioter and dropped him to the floor in a much more cooperative attitude. Within minutes, 40 Marines were sitting on the floor, moaning in pain as they gripped their aching lower legs.

Sergeant Lauterbach was dumbfounded. "Geez, you guys laid out the whole bunch!" he gasped.

Carl eyed him sourly. "Yeah. Well, now we've got to lock these guys up. Somebody's gonna have a pretty good bill to pay."

As the interior became quieter, five round Chinese faces appeared from behind the bar and we were beset with five shrill voices screeching at us in Mandarin. "Look, we're going to lock these guys up in the Army jail! " Carl yelled at the five Orientals. "You can go down tomorrow and file charges."

The Chinese bartenders kept wanting to explain how the fight started but we couldn't understand them and didn't much care. We just wanted to clear up the mess and get back to our job at Tondeleyo's before things came unhinged down there. The Marine Corps didn't have a jail in Honakaa, but the U.S Army Provost had an office and a brig a block away. So Carl and I escorted the limping combatants, two or three at a time, to the Army pokey where they would be secure for the night. Ed and another disheveled MP stood guard over the rest who were still sitting on the floor holding their legs. Ed accompanied us with the last two, rubbing his right eye, which was now getting purple. Carl lashed into him for letting the situation get out of control and Ed answered with a couple of smart remarks in return which set Carl's teeth on edge.

As we booked the final two rioters and turned to go, the Army Provost aimed a finger at Lauterbach, noting the black eye and torn shirt. "What about him?" he asked.

"I'm one of the Marine M P.'s," Ed explained.

"Is he with you guys?" the Provost asked.

I was dumbfounded to hear Carl say: "Never saw this drunk before in my life."

Two Army M P.'s grabbed Lauterbach, who struggled and protested as they dragged him to the bull pen and slammed the door shut.

When I got my voice back, I said: "Geez, Carl, that was a lousy trick. Earl's locked up with all those drunks and he doesn't even drink. He can't even stand the smell of alcohol."

"That's what's so darn funny," Carl laughed. "Besides, he caused us a whole lot of grief. Let's get back to Tondeleyo's before we have another riot."

I had to go down to the Army jail in the morning with the company commander while charges were filed against the rioters. I got Ed out, explaining to the Army Provost that a mistake had been made; but Ed was so mad he wouldn't even speak to

126

me. Fact is, he didn't speak to either Carl or me until weeks later when we were on board ship, heading for Saipan. Lauterbach was a nice guy and a good sergeant. And it was a lousy trick Houston played on him.

But it was funny.

Chapter 15
Pearl Harbor No. 2

Every kid who attends public school is aware of something called "Pearl Harbor" which occurred in Hawaii on Dec. 7, although they may no longer know it was in 1941. However, hardly anybody knows about the ships sunk at the Second Pearl Harbor, except those of us who were there. It was hushed up because the government didn't want the enemy to know about it. Also, the Japanese didn't do it. We did it to ourselves.

May 21, 1944, dawned warm and clear in Hawaii. The wreck of the battleship Arizona and parts of other ships sunk by the Japanese attack were visible jutting from the slick, calm surface at Pearl. We were loading up to go again, exactly where we weren't sure, but a logical target seemed the Marianas, a base closer to mainland Japan. We were pretty well recovered from Tarawa and Guadalcanal. Many gaps had been filled in the ranks even though 95% of the Guadalcanal veterans were still subject to periodic bouts of malaria. Equipment had been replaced and we were hot to go. One difference: We were going on LST's, which stood for Landing Ship Tank. These were huge steel boxes, flat-bottomed, with shallow draft and equipped with a bow door that flopped down so we could drive tanks, trucks or anything else right off the forward ramp onto the beach. The concept was that these craft could travel fully loaded in a task force and deliver troops and equipment right to the shore. No loading or unloading transports in a bay where enemy aircraft could wreak havoc. The one problem was that we had vehicles, weapons, cases of ammunition, explosives and drums of gasoline all jammed together in the hold. A spark down there and the ship would go up like a huge firecracker. Each LST was, in effect, a floating bomb.

At mid-morning, I was standing on the bow of LST 262 in charge of a crew loading munitions, drums of gasoline and other highly flammable items through the huge bow door. In the distance, sailors in their whites were in small boats heading for shore leave in Honolulu. Other small boats were bringing out supplies and returning to shore empty. Big, white seagulls wheeled overhead, screeching. Below my post on the bow was a mixed crew of Marines and Sailors moving crates and drums along with cloverleaves of cannon ammo. Like the other LST's in this huge flotilla anchored in Pearl Harbor, we were lashed together in groups of five like firecrackers with a short space of water between our five and the next, enough space to allow small cargo craft to maneuver. Our craft was in the middle of five with two other LST's on the port and starboard.

Everything was going smoothly until an explosion occurred on an LST two groups ahead of ours. There was a heck of a boom and a column of smoke shot up from the ship's hatch. The crew below me jumped and looked up with startled looks. "What's going on, Sarge?" somebody yelled.

"Looks like somebody had an accident," I yelled back. It turned out that an elevator slipped carrying pyrotechnics (flares) from the upper deck down into the hold. Just let go and crashed into the hold.

There was a pause as smoke continued to drift out of the hatch and then the whole center section of the deck blew up and flames licked the superstructure. "Secure the loading party!" I yelled at the crew below, but that order wasn't really necessary. They were already buttoning up the project and the big bow door was grinding to the closed position. The Navy cargo boats were starting to back away and head for safety. At that point, the burning LST suddenly blew to pieces. The bow and stern vanished in a balloon of flame. Burning hunks of the super structure went flying through the air along with what looked like people. Then the two LST's on either side of the first one began to burn and I could see Marines and sailors running around on the decks, some hosing water on the fires and others jumping into the sea. And then the second two burning LST's exploded with tremendous bangs. Fragments of burning material landed on our deck along with smoking hot chunks of steel. Some of us on the deck ducked for protection under the steel gun turrets. Sailors yanked hoses loose and began spraying water on the smoking debris.

Luckily, our ship's commander was on board, not loafing ashore or playing golf at Honolulu. He hit the deck running, barking orders, and had crewmen chopping the lines loose that secured us to the other LST's, port and starboard. At the same time he issued orders to the engine room for full speed astern. As we backed slowly away from the mess, two more LST's, directly in front of us, caught fire. Our crew was hosing down the deck, making sure the hissing pieces of burning material and red hot hunks of steel clanging down from the sky didn't start our craft afire. Those of us on deck, other than the crew manning hoses, stayed under the cover of the gun turrets. We could see small boats dashing about in the wreckage picking up survivors from the water and we could see frantic activity on board the rest of the LST fleet. By the time we had backed well out into the main area of Pearl Harbor and away from trouble, at least five or six LST's had blown to smithereens and some others were belching smoke. The official report was that five sank, but it looked like more than that blew up. We were told we could not write home about the accident and not discuss it if we were ashore. They didn't want the Japanese to know we had a problem but the Japs probably knew all about it. Of course, none of us got ashore to talk about it, anyway. However, it was an ill omen for our part of a task force getting ready to sail. And this came on the heels of another, smaller disaster. Just before that, we were involved in maneuvers off the island of Maui and were caught in a typhoon. It was one heck of a blow and all the fleet of LST's could do was head right into it and try to hold position without banging into one another. The seas were huge, breaking over the bows of the ships and smacking against the superstructures and the gun turrets. Sergeant Carl Houston and I had been on deck duty manning anti-aircraft weapons when the blow hit, so we stayed above decks to watch the show.

"Let's go topside and see what it looks like from the LCI," he yelled over the roar of the storm. On the top deck of each LST, riding piggy-back, rested an LCT or LCI, which were Landing Craft Tank or Landing Craft Infantry, smaller variations of the same front ramp steel boxes composing the LST's. A whole company of tanks or foot troops could be packed inside and delivered directly to the beach. Although these smaller craft looked unwieldy sitting on the top deck of an LST, they were locked in place with steel braces welded to the hull of the mother ship. At the landing site, the steel braces would be cut with a torch, the deck of the LST tilted, and the LCI or LCT skidded off into the water..

In the storm's roar, with billows of foam washing down the deck of LST 262, Houston and I scrambled up a steel ladder to the top of the LCI from where we had a magnificent view of the raging typhoon. Our ship was not only half submerged every

132

time it plowed through a huge wave, but it also rocked side to side at a about a 45 degree tilt. We had a ride you couldn't buy at any amusement park.

Within minutes, we lost sight of the other ships in the flotilla as we simply plunged ahead into the waves. By dark, the storm was beginning to subside so Houston and I climbed down from our observation perch and went into the ship's galley for a sandwich and hot coffee. We didn't feel any particular concern over the storm, figuring the LST was seaworthy and could ride it out just fine plus the Navy crew knew their business. We didn't find out until the next day that the waves had knocked three LCI's from the decks of three other LST's and took with them some 30 Marines who were above decks like Houston and I. Those 30 Marines simply vanished into the Pacific Ocean. Maybe Carl and I were luckier than we thought.

In any event, following the storm, the fire and exploding craft, Task Force 58 was finally assembled, loaded and shipped out from Pearl on May 25. All day, the bigger transports, carriers and other ships were threading their way past the wreckage of the Arizona and other mementos of Dec 7. Our flotilla of LSTs didn't get moving until sunset. As we headed slowly toward open sea, 12 long, black submarines churned past us, up close on the surface. Frankly, we had never seen anything more deadly-looking in the water and we stood on the deck in awe staring at these cigar-shaped, quiet weapons of destruction. As the last one moved away leaving a small wake of foam, somebody on our LST echoed our sentiments: "Geez, I am sure glad those are ours!"

And somebody else said: "Amen!"

We hit the open sea as the sun skidded below the horizon. The whole ocean seemed alive with ships as far as we could see - aircraft carriers, battleships, cruisers, destroyers, mine sweepers, transports and the big mass of steel boxes, the LST's. There was not a whole lot of talk. Some Marines sat on deck, oiling their rifles for the umpteenth time. Some methodically sharpened bayonets or belt knives. Some smoked cigarettes. All eyes were mainly on the western horizon, alight with an orange glow. Somewhere out there was a big Japanese base with ships, bombers, fighter planes, shore batteries, tanks and ground troops. We wondered if they knew we were coming and we wondered how good they were. We knew how good we were and we knew we were on our way to destroy them. We were like a well-coached unbeaten football team, eager to keep our winning streak intact.

Waves broke away from the bow of our LST sending streamers of foam toward the stern. Periodically, small clusters of flying fish skipped over the water surface from one wave to the next, like bluish-silver streaks. Here and there, Marines were reading tattered paperback books. A few were writing letters home. Others just sat and stared at the horizon. From the number of ships in task Force 58 - some 500 we were told - it was apparent that we were going into something really big. How big, we were to find out a few days later when we were briefed in the hold of the ship. Our destination was Saipan in the Mariana Islands, the Japanese main Pacific base. It was within air range of Japan itself and the last step to the Island of Okinawa, jump-off point for the invasion of the Japanese homeland.

We were on the downhill run. The war was winding down in the Pacific and the Second Marine Division was one of the reasons. We all knew hell lay ahead, but we were in high gear for the attack. The Japanese navy was all but beaten. The Japanese air force was in shot to pieces. They still had a lot of ground troops left but we knew their game plan. We had their playbook and we knew everything they did and how to defeat them. We were tested, experienced and tough. We were darn good and we knew it.

Chapter 16
Going In

There is a lot to think about in an invasion. The task force - troopships, battleships, cruisers, destroyers, submarines and aircraft carriers - is involved in getting the troops and supplies to the target intact, in wrecking as much of the enemy's defenses as possible and of protecting the task force from counter-attack. The division has the problem making sure every regiment has the necessary trucks, jeeps, gasoline, weapons, ammunition, food and even toilet paper. The division also has the problem of making sure every regimental commander understands the mission and they, in turn, brief the battalion commanders who brief the company commanders who go over every detail with the platoon leaders. Everyone, down to the last private in every squad, knows the mission. That is why Marine units which lose regimental, battalion and company commanders can keep right on fighting. The next guy down steps up to take over.

An attack is planned in stages with each regiment having a

specific goal mapped for each day. The maps show D-day, D plus 1, D plus 2 and so on until the mission is completed. In the Marine Corps there is no provision for failure. There is no provision for retreat. There is only attack. Everyone down to the last private knows this and it is that which makes the U.S. Marine Corps so formidable.

Even in boot camp, this was drilled into our heads. In a session involving bugle calls, we had to identify the call for reveille, dinner, pay call, colors and taps. "What is the bugle call for retreat?" the drill sergeant asked, looking intently at each of us.

Receiving no answer, he bellowed: "There is none in the Marine Corps! Nor is there any call for surrender. If you are outnumbered 10-to-one, out of ammunition and the situation is hopeless, you fix bayonets, charge straight into the enemy and take out as many as you can!"

It was the mindset of every member of the Second Division as we watched the morning bombardment of Saipan from the decks of the troop ship. Not only were all the warships pumping ordnance at the island, but also dive-bombers were howling in like a swam of bees, plastering communications, trucks and supply dumps. The whole beach section was a pall of smoke and flying dirt. Huge black clouds erupted from fuel and ammo dumps and from the shell-torn towns of Garapan and Charan Kanoa.

Corporal Jim Lowe came up and murmured in my ear: "We found it."

"O.K.," I looked around to make sure we weren't being overheard. "Where is it?"

Jim motioned to follow. The rest of the squad looked at us and I signaled for half the men to come along. All the sailors in the ship's crew were on deck busy watching the bombardment. It was their first combat operation and they were understandably excited. What we were doing, in the meantime, was taking care of our own survival.

The night before we had been issued our food rations for

the first couple of days ashore. These were in small, waxed paper cartons marked "K Ration." They contained some dry crackers that looked and tasted like compressed cardboard and some tiny tins of cheese or meat product to spread on the cracker. Also enclosed was a packet of something like Kool Aid but was not only poorly flavored but usually rendered by tropical heat into a hard chip that would not dissolve. We noticed that it was packed for the military by the Alka-Seltzer Co. at Elkhart, Indiana. We would have been a lot better off with Alka Seltzer. Lastly, the ration box contained three moldy cigarettes. More tropical effects. The cigarettes were green on the ends and tasted like burnt sox.

At the squad meeting the night before, we decided to have Lowe and a couple others slip into the ship's galley when the crew was busy above decks and see if they could locate the locker where canned fruit and fruit juice were stored. It didn't take Jim and his searchers long to hit the jackpot.

A few men at a time, to not attract attention, we filed down to the galley, threw out our K Rations and other extraneous gear and filled our packsacks with canned peaches, pears, plums, fruit cocktail, orange juice, apple juice and whatever else struck our fancy, like Saltine crackers. It made our packs considerably heavier but we reasoned that if we were going to get shot, we at least would go out with something better than K Rations in our guts.

We came back on deck to watch lines of amphibian tractors heading for the beach. Like Tarawa, there was a coral reef some distance off shore that tractors had to climb up and over. We had heard that some new amphibian tanks with 75mm cannons were in the first wave, but we couldn't see them from the deck. We could see some rocket boats moving in and we could also see white waterspouts where Jap shells were trying to target the amphibs. A few vehicles were stalled out on the reef. It was apparent that not all of the Jap shells were off the mark.

Corporal Larry Zinck was on the rail to my right. "You know what today is?" I asked.

"Yeah, June 15," said Larry.

"You know what June 15 is back home in Illinois?"

Larry looked mystified. "What is it, Sarge?"

"June 15 is opening day of the bass fishing season and I wish I was fishing on the Fox River back home."

Larry looked at the carnage on the beach for a second: "I wish we were both fishing on the Fox River," he said softly.

At this point, the First Sergeant bawled across the deck: "O. K., men! Time to go to work!"

We headed down the steel ladders to the hold where the LST ramp door was grinding open. The heavily-loaded amtracs began clanking across the steel deck, then splashed off into the water. Amid shouts of orders, bits and pieces of conversation drifted over the group. Our radiomen had been in contact with Lt. Wyer who had gone in with the first wave to scout out and set up an advanced artillery fire control post. Wyer had called over the radio in his deep southern drawl to say that his amtrac team had taken a hand grenade when it landed on the beach and suffered several casualties. "Ah have been hit," Wyer stated, flatly," but ah believe ah will be able to continue." He said he was heading inland with a rifle squad and would report again. It was clear that the enemy was providing a welcoming party on the beach like we thought they would.

Our wave of amtracs fanned out in a bobbing line, then, on signal, started for the beach, engines wide open. Squad leaders had our heads above the gunwales, studying the beach ahead. The wall of smoke and dirt was still flying high in the air, but now it wasn't from our Naval guns and dive bombers. It was all their stuff, all Japanese artillery. As we got closer, we could see amtracs, halftracks and tanks along the beach, some tipped over, some on fire. Some armored tractors with 75mm guns were firing inland and several of those appeared damaged. Jap shells began landing around our little fleet of amtracs, pieces of steel rattled off the hulls. I lowered my head until my eyes were just even with the gunwale. I wanted to keep track of everything we were heading into. Somewhere beyond the beach I knew, we had to cross a concrete air strip and move in on the left of a Jap sugar mill near a swamp named on the map as Lake Susupe.

Some of the landing craft, like ours, had small steel turrets on the deck with slits for the drivers to peer through. As the shore fire grew more intense, some of the coxswains began to slam the steel covers shut over the slits, lost their direction and began to wander off course. Some got fairly well off course and blundered into other landing zones, creating chaos on the beach. Some we saw wander south toward the beaches near Charan Kanoa where the Fourth Division was supposed to be landing. In the tangle, the Fourth didn't get to shore at the village, but a few of our amtracs did, right in the middle of the Jap defenses. With apprehension, I watched three amtracs go astray, one of them carrying the squad, which included my good buddy Corp. William Bell. I knew with grim certainty that Bell was a goner but I knew he and the squad would put up a heck of a fight as long as they lasted.

Inexorably, the smoking, hellish beach approached. Corporal Zinck had the map case with our first night's command post location. I told him to stick to me like glue no matter what. He nodded with narrowed eyes, licked his lips and gripped his rifle. The last thing I saw before we hit the sand was more busted machines inland and some wounded and dead Marines.

"When this thing hits, bail out and scatter!" I hissed at the squad. "Get the hell off the beach! It's a death trap!"

The men looked at me. Some of the hard-jawed old timers nodded. Some of the new ones were pale and sweating, but still ready to go.

Whoomp! The steel tracks hit the sand and we were ashore. The amtrac tilted up for a second and then dropped with a thud into a huge shell hole and stalled. That was a break because when we went over the side, the shell hole provided some protection from the roaring, dirt-laced bedlam around us. I motioned to Zinck to follow, jumped out of the shell hole and sprinted down the beach to the right. The Japs had us well bracketed with artillery and mortars which were coming down in a near-continuous roar. On top of that, stray machine gun fire chipped at the few standing coconut trees as we scooted toward the south looking for an avenue inland. A short distance away I spotted one of our men face down in the sand. He was yelling: "I'm hit ! I'm hit!" Zinck and I slid up alongside the guy. It was PFC Pete Larson. He was spooked, pale and sweating, but I couldn't see any blood.

"Where're you hit?" I hollered in his ear.

"I'm' hit in the butt!" he cried.

I looked at him and realized a Jap rifle bullet had drilled his canteen. With the bullet's impact and the warm water leaking out, Larson thought he was bleeding to death. I tried to keep from laughing as I yelled the situation in his ear. He reached around to grab the canteen, looked sheepish but relieved, and took off running. Next I spotted the opening to a sandbagged Jap dugout. I skidded up close and dove for the opening...to find myself staring into the muzzle of a Jap .256 Nambu machinegun. A Jap soldier was sitting erect directly behind it. My blood froze for a second until it registered that the Jap had a bullet hole in his forehead and was extremely dead. Taking a deep breath, I took off at a sprint heading inland toward the concrete air strip, Zinck on my heels. I knew we had to cross the airstrip and move about 400 yards beyond to our designated position.

The airstrip was an inferno of deafening noise - artillery fire, mortar fire, flying concrete and dust. There was wrecked equipment and dead Marines as far as we could see to the right and left. Although it was less than 100 yards across the strip, Larry and I skidded into a shell hole to assess the situation. The trouble with the concrete strip was that the Japs on the hills above us could see a gnat walking across it and could pinpoint fire on any square yard. Also, when a shell hit the concrete it sent a hail of steel fragments flying at knee height, like a giant mowing machine.

Then, for no apparent reason, the Jap barrage lifted. Perhaps they paused, waiting for the smoke to clear so they could spot more targets. "Go!" I yelled at Larry and we hit the airstrip on a dead run. Just as we reached the trees on the other side the Japs opened up again and Marines coming behind us ran into a hail of shellfire. Larry and I continued through a standing grove of coconut trees, running at a half crouch, using any cover we could find. I had some landmarks picked out, such as the smokestack on the sugar mill, and kept these in view as we headed for the proposed command post, a farmyard near a crossroad.

Eventually, we ducked and crawled to where we could see our goal. A Marine with a smoking Garand was resting on his elbows behind a clump of cedar brush. I slid up alongside him and pointed to the spot on the map and the buildings ahead. "Is that the farm yard?"

He nodded and grinned a little. "Yeah, but you can't go there."

"Why not?"

"We don't own it yet," With that he dropped his cheek back on the stock of the Garand and watched for movement. Then we spotted two of our battalion officers and some enlisted personnel dodging toward the farm buildings from the left. They sprinted toward the farm, so Larry and I took off, too. No live Jap defenders were evident. The first floor of the farmhouse was blown away but the foundation was intact, located about five feet below ground level. With this cover, we immediately organized radio communications with the three batteries setting up in the trees nearby and prepared to get some fire missions going in support of the infantry units ahead and to our right.

The radio crackled and Lt. Wyer's voice came on: "Ah have been hit again." He gave the map coordinates where he was located which was only a few hundred yards away. He said a Jap sniper had shot him in the hand while he was looking through his field glasses and the bullet was stuck in the base of his thumb. "Mah thumb hit mah eye and ah believe ah am gettin' a black eye," he laughed. A few minutes later he called in to say he had been hit again, this time in the legs. "Ah do not feel capable of carrying on much longer, but ah will man the radio until someone shows up to relieve me." The Colonel sent another forward observation spotter to relieve Wyer and instructed a runner to locate a Jeep to haul Wyer down to the beach for medical aid.

Although the shellfire around the farmyard was not as intense as on the beach, it was noisy enough to make communications difficult. To be heard, we had to yell into the hand set. Eventually, the rest of the battalion command arrived at the farmhouse foundation and we became better organized. We had suffered relatively few casualties, unlike some of the regiments, which lost many of their top people.

The batteries were set up and we got a few fire missions on the way when the Japs began combing the coconut groves with artillery fire, trying to quiet us down. They had good observation posts on the hills overlooking us and could see every move we made. But that didn't totally account for the pinpoint accuracy of their artillery fire. The problem related to the confusion of the landing and the gap between the Second Division and the Fourth Division at the village of Charan Kanoa. The Japs still held the village although Naval gunfire had reduced it to a jumble of concrete and tin roofing. The big sugar mill had been flattened with one exception - the towering brick smokestack was still standing. Somebody, listening to radio signals, guessed correctly that there was a Jap observer in the top of the smokestack who was calling in the artillery fire. Division command called for air support to blow up the smokestack. Several dive-bombers off the carriers came in and unloaded, but couldn't seem to hit the target. Over the radio we could hear all kinds of cross-communication going on: "Get that damn smokestack down!" somebody was screaming. "The guy in there is killing us!"

Finally, a torpedo plane came in low and let go, but the torpedo skipped and nearly skidded into our own people. With that, a rifle squad charged the sugar mill and somebody fired an automatic rifle up the stack, silencing our tormentor.

While Larry Zinck had carried the map case with some vital charts, our big map case with large-scale maps of the whole island was being packed in by Corporal Simmons. Nobody had seen Simmons since the landing and no one knew if he was still alive until he suddenly appeared during a heavy mortar barrage. Dozens of 81mm mortar shells were crashing in around the farmhouse when somebody spotted Simmons darting through the coconut trees to come sliding under a nearby building that was up on three-foot posts. We yelled at him and he signaled he saw us. When there was a lull in the barrage, he came zigzagging toward us on a dead run.

The thing was, all Japanese farmers saved their poop for fertilizer. Stuff they called "night soil." They had open outside toilets built with concrete troughs. The human waste ran down the troughs into big cesspools where it was allowed to "age" before being spread on the farm. Some of these "aging" pools acquired a thick green scum over the top that looked like grass. Simmons took a short cut across one of these and vanished with a great splash. He went clear under but his right hand stayed above the surface holding the map case aloft. In a second, he scrambled out of the cesspool, dripping black slime, sputtering and gagging, but with the map case intact. Three more mortars exploded in the yard as Simmons slid on his belly to a window opening, shoved the map case into the farmhouse foundation and started to follow it in. At this point First Sergeant Bittick put his boot against Simmon's chest and shoved him back.

143

"You ain't coming in here stinking like that!" he yelled.

Another mortar went off in the yard and Simmons looked terrified. But he was more scared of the First Sergeant. He leaped up and dashed frantically back across the yard to the building he just left, slid under it and passed out of sight.

"That was a lousy thing to do," somebody yelled at the First Sergeant.

"Yeah? Well it's one thing to get shot and it is another to die from stink," Bittick said.

Actually, the farmhouse foundation was not a very good command post. It was too big and invited a couple of mortar or artillery shells to land inside and wipe out everybody. Col. Shell didn't like it. He also figured the Japs could see it all too plainly from their observation posts on the hills, had it targeted on their maps and would eventually open up on us. He ordered a new command post to be dug in a nearby grove of trees a hundred yards away and sent a detail out to accomplish it. Shell was right. We got a Fire Control pit dug, a smaller communications pit dug and the equipment moved just before three 90 mm shells crashed inside the spot we had just left. The difference between life and death had narrowed down to a few seconds and there was no room for error.

By now, we not only had our Howitzers registered and firing, but all extra personnel were digging in for the coming night. Machine guns were set in place on the flanks with protecting riflemen. Everyone had a supply of grenades. We fully expected the enemy would come with a massive counterattack as soon as it was dark. What we didn't know was that our Naval fire and dive bombers had so disrupted the enemy communications and so fragmented their troops that it took all that night and most of the next day to get a coordinated attack organized. That was lucky because we were pretty much a mess on D-day. Over the radio we heard there were some sporadic attacks on our left. "Guess what?" a radioman said: "The Nips came running right

144

up the coast road in formation from Garapan and ran head-on into the Sixth. Wiped 'em out."

But not in our sector. There was some infiltrating and sniper fire but no massive land attack. However, the Jap artillery fire grew intense with some huge projectiles howling in. Sixteen-inch shore batteries up the coast toward Garapan began hurling some deafening stuff at us. The scuttlebutt was that these were shore guns the Japs had captured from the British at Singapore, hauled them down by ship and installed them to guard Saipan. They were the noisiest weapons we had run into so far. We knew they were 16-inchers because a couple of them didn't go off. These duds howled in, whumped on the dirt, skidded in a cloud of dust and stopped, lying on top of the ground like big, deadly, steel cylinders waiting to blow somebody's head off.

Twice when runners were sent to carry messages to the firing batteries, they made wide detours around those duds like their footsteps might set them off. All together, a couple dozen of those 16-inchers came howling down the coast like boxcars going end-for-end. When they exploded, the whole island shook. In our foxholes, we flattened out with our forearms under us so we could raise our bodies up a couple of inches off the ground before the shell hit. To take the impact directly to the stomach could have meant getting our guts smashed.

Just before dark an airplane came over the treetops and we ducked, but it was one of ours. It looked like a dive-bomber. The pilot made several low level passes with his flaps down and it became apparent he was trying to land on the little concrete fighter strip we had just crossed. "He can't get that thing in there," somebody said. But evidently the pilot had been given orders to land on that strip. He finally mushed in, throttle back and hit the concrete riding his brakes. There simply wasn't enough strip. He screeched into the trees at the end and exploded. Even after all we had seen on the beach, we were horror-struck at this one. "They will probably send a letter to his family saying he died for his country in combat," somebody said. "Not that some jackass ordered him to land on a strip that was too small."

And that wasn't all the idiocy. Right after that, six little observation planes that looked like Piper Cubs came in and did land. Somebody in the military hierarchy had determined that we could use some low level aerial observation aircraft, ordinarily a good idea; but sending the planes in when we had just gotten the strip was a bad idea. The pilots taxied their planes to a nice line on runway and then ran for cover as the Jap artillery opened up again. Within 20 minutes all that was left of the six observation planes were the frames and engines. We sometimes wondered who came up some of those wizard ideas.

All night the shelling continued and some of our people were getting hit. The problem was, the fire was so intense, we couldn't get our wounded to the beach and nobody from the beach could get to us. A few yards from the command post was PFC Wolfe in his foxhole. Wolfe was a little guy, funnier than the dickens. The word was he was learning how to be a stand up comic before the war. Even under fire, Wolfe had something funny to say. Until one incoming shell hit a tree overhead and exploded, sending steel fragments ripping into him. When he came to, he started yelling for the corpsman who crawled over but couldn't do much. Wolfe's screams got louder and then began to weaken. Eventually, all we could hear was the little guy sobbing: "Mom! Mom!" It was a god-awful night. By daylight, Wolfe was dead.

But daylight brought some benefits. Most of us were surprised to be still alive and functioning. The battalion was shooting, in spite of Jap fire which had disabled some of our artillery pieces and knocked some gun crews out of action. We began to evacuate our wounded although it was too late to do anything for Wolfe. Supplies began coming in. The best thing was, we had time to get organized, to straighten out and strengthen our defenses, get more weapons and troops ashore and brace for the counter attack.

Col. Shell had us lay a coconut log-and-sandbag roof over the command post and communications pit so we could operate at night with flashlights and not be spotted by Jap observers. We also got a much-needed first aid pit dug in to provide shelter for the doctor and the medics while they were working on the wounded.

The high point of the morning was the arrival of two bullet-scarred jeeps from up the coast toward Charan Kanoa. Standing up in the lead jeep, gripping the windshield with one bandaged, bloody hand and waving a huge Jap samurai sword in the other was Corporal Bell, yelling: "Follow me, men!"

Some of us ran over to the jeep, laughing, and somebody said: "Geez, Bell, we saw your amtrac go off course. We thought you were dead."

"So did I!" Bell laughed. "We landed inside the Jap lines and they were as surprised as we were. We tore up the beach on the dead run while they fired at us. We got nicked, but nobody got killed." There was something to be said for lousy Jap marksmanship.

As evening came on, it was apparent the counterattack was coming. There was a lot of activity observed on the hills across from our position and along Lake Susupe. The Fourth Division had entered Charan Kanoa but there was still a gap between the Second and the Fourth divisions. Col. Shell was in contact with Division and wanted to know what the heck was going on. As near as he could determine, the Fourth Division Commander requested that the Second Division moves to its right to fill the gap. Our Division Commander, General Watson, requested that the Fourth move to its left and fill the gap. Even the report that the Army 27th Division was being committed in the Fourth Division area and that overall battle commander, General Holland M. (Howlin' Mad) Smith had come ashore, did not correct the problem. Night came on with the gap near Charan Kanoa unresolved. While Headquarters Company opened packages of K Rations and bitched, my squad cracked open half gallon cans of fruit and fruit juice.

Then we hunkered down for a heck of a fight.

Chapter 17

Earning Our Pay

Marines get paid to fight. The night of D-plus-1 on Saipan, we began to earn our money. Sporadically, Jap artillery raked over our positions, moving up and down the lines and back to the beach with regularity and with some accuracy. Our 75mm peashooters were firing back as fast as the crews could load, but the enemy stuff was a lot bigger and their observation was much better. They were on target a lot of the time. Some of our guns were knocked out and the crews with them.

Up and down the front, Jap infantry probed our defenses looking for soft spots. The gap between the Second Division and the Fourth was exploited and we were having trouble on that flank. Sometime during the night there was a lull and we heard the sound of engines. A lot of engines. Word came in over the radio to prepare for a Jap tank attack. The Navy kept firing star shells over the area, keeping the place lit up like day. The burning flares drifted in the breeze so the scene was continually changing, the shadows of the trees moving as the flares moved. This was spooky because these moving shadows sometimes looked like Japs slipping through the coconut groves.

The sound of Jap tank engines revving up got louder to our left. Still, there was no firing, a puzzling development as the tanks clanked through where the Sixth Regiment was supposed to be dug in. Finally, the Jap tanks stopped behind and to our left, between our lines and the beach. What happened, according to some of the guys we talked to later, the Jarheads of the Sixth Regiment spotted the tanks coming and were ordered to hold their fire and wait for the infantry expected to be coming behind them. As the tanks rolled up, the Marines had near-perfect fire discipline, just sitting tight as the Japs ran right over their positions. Not receiving any fire baffled the Jap tankers who advanced several hundred yards, figured there should have been some shooting and stopped to look around.

At that point, their world came apart in the dark. Sixth Regiment Marine bazooka teams and automatic riflemen had trailed the Jap tanks to the trees where they pulled up. It was a turkey shoot. Point blank, rockets from the bazookas tore into the lightly-armored sides of the tanks and blew them sky-high. Some Japs tried to climb out and were blown off the turrets by BAR-men. Between 30 and 40 Jap tanks went up in smoke. Only three managed to get going and lumbered back to the safety of their lines.

A couple of Sixth Regiment riflemen said it was pretty hairy watching the Jap tanks roll right a over the foxholes, the tank treads rumbling overhead. But the Jap ground attack was not well coordinated. There was a gap in time before their infantry came screaming and ran right into our machine guns, rifles and 37mm field weapons. The First Battalion, 10th Marines, also on our left in direct support of the Sixth, was loading and firing their 75mm guns point blank into the Jap infantry. They even managed to bore sight and crack off several rounds at the Jap tanks.

Hordes of screaming Japanese hit all along the line, a few

breaking through near some of our batteries. But our lines generally held firm. Repulsed, the Japs opened up again with artillery. Our battalion communications dugout was busy fielding requests for fire support and sending firing orders to whatever guns were sill functioning. The Jap artillery fire got so noisy, we had to drag our telephone switchboard into the connecting trench between the communication pit and the command post in order to relay the firing commands. I was sitting with my legs under the switchboard. Operating with a flashlight in one hand. PFC Pete Niblo was on the field phone receiving the forward OP target data PFC Bates was at my elbow in the connecting trench relaying orders over the crash of Jap artillery to the men in the CP who were working on maps and firing charts.

The enemy obviously had our position pretty well pinpointed. Some heavy stuff went off just outside, showering the CP with dirt and rocks. Every time one came close we hunched up and kind of ducked our heads as if this would provide some kind of protection. Then they had us bracketed with overs and shorts. Being artillerymen, we knew the drill. Now they would split the bracket and drop some in the middle. We tensed up as the first of several incomers landed on us.

One blew out the back of the communication pit but didn't do anything except shake us up. Then one came screeching in, hit the coconut log roof and blew it away. That was a deafening impact. When I came to, I could not feel anything. Nothing. I figured I was dead and that was what dead felt like. It was as if I was floating horizontally in space except with the roof gone, I could now see the stars in the night sky. The switchboard was on my lap and Bates underneath me was coughing and groaning: "My chest! My chest!"

"This is ridiculous." I thought, "Bates is beefing about his damn chest and here I am dead!"

Then, feeling slowly came into my body, creeping up my arms and legs. It was the same sensation as when you hit your crazy bone, only all over. PFC Bates, under me, shifted around and emerged from the dirt, still coughing and spitting. There were some groans in the command post and then the dirt in the connecting trench heaved up and Pete Niblo appeared gripping the telephone hand set. He held it toward the light and we could see the wire had been blown away with maybe a foot of it left dangling. Pete put the handset up to his head and yelled to nobody in particular: "This is PFC Niblo securing this set! Over and out!" and hurled the handset into the night.

We thought the Japs would follow up with some more shells, now they had us targeted, but maybe they figured they got us. There was a lull and we got the injured to the first aid pit and set about trying to rebuild the command post. The battalion was not firing anyway because none of the batteries were in condition to fire. They had all been knocked out. Slowly we got the shattered logs and sandbag pieces collected, the two pits and connecting trench back in operating order. About then, Captain Morgan, the battalion communications officer came running over to see who was functioning. "Come on!" he yelled, waving his carbine. "The Japs broke through on the right! We got to plug that gap or they will get behind us on the beach!"

A dozen volunteers came up from the dirt with rifles and grenades. When I went on duty I had laid my rifle on the rim of the connecting trench. Now I reached up and it was gone. I crawled out and spotted it eight feet away, but the wooden stock was blown in half. Captain Morgan was yelling at us to get a move on and I hollered back that the stock was blown off my rifle.

"Find another one!" he yelled. "There's got to be some lying around."

I took off with him and the other guys, threading our way through ripped up coconut trees, strands of barbed wire and assorted debris. Navy star shells kept the place well lighted as we dodged through the rubble. I kept looking for a rifle but couldn't see one.

"Here!" Morgan yelled, pointing his carbine at some vacant foxholes overlooking an opening. It was where the Japs had overrun a squad and broken through. A half dozen dead Marines and Japs were scattered on the ground. "Hold this position!" Morgan bellowed and took off looking for reinforcements.

How it happened, I do no know but I wound up the farthest Marine forward in the line of foxholes. I had several grenades and my sheath knife, but no rifle. A Marine without his rifle is like a preacher without his pants. However, I figured if they came I could hurl grenades while the riflemen did their work. We were still somewhat stunned and disorganized from the artillery shells that hit the Command Post and not really too alert, but we were going to make any Japs pay if they tried to exploit the breakthrough. Enemy artillery was still howling in, but had shifted 200 yards behind us, probably to avoid hitting their own men. It was relatively quiet where we were hunkered down, intently watching the shadows move around as the flares drifted.

Then I spotted a moving shadow that didn't belong to a tree or bush. Fifty yards away, there was a soldier crawling toward me, sliding from foxhole to foxhole, pausing for a few seconds in each hole to look around. He was coming toward me at an angle and looked to come within 15 feet.

The nearest member of our team with a rifle was Sgt. Lauterbach in the next foxhole. Lauterbach was tough and a dead shot. He had a rifle and I didn't. I whispered as loud as I could: "Lauterbach! Throw me your rifle!"

"Like hell!" he hissed back.

"Listen, I got one coming in," I said. "Let me nail him and I'll throw the rifle back."

Lauterbach raised up a little then pitched his rifle toward me. I caught it and turned around to keep track of the target. The guy kept crawling toward me, foxhole to foxhole. It was going to be an easy shot. I braced the rifle on the edge of the hole, balanced on my elbows and drew a bead. I could see the top of his helmet moving closer. He was carrying a rifle with bayonet on the end and he had no idea anyone was watching him. When he was only about 15 feet away I could see him clearly and figured to put him away with one shot in the head. I slipped off the safety and slid my forefinger against the trigger as he slowly raised up to look around. He was lit up brightly by a flare and as his helmet cleared the edge of the hole, I laid the bead right on his ear. And then I sensed something wrong. He was wearing a G.I. helmet, not Japanese. This was nothing new because the Japs often infiltrated wearing our gear, but this seemed different. I picked up a clod of mud, threw it at the guy. It hit next to him and he pulled his head down. Then he raised way up and looked around. I could see it was no Jap. I pulled my finger out of the trigger guard and felt a trickle of cold sweat run down my neck. I realized I darn near shot one of our own!

"Hey!" I called to the guy,

He jumped and turned toward me.

"You almost got shot !" I rasped.

"Where am I?" the guy asked.

"What outfit are you with" I fired back.

"Twenty-ninth. We had a heck of a bayonet fight and I don't know who's left alive. We couldn't hold the hill and I don't think there were any Japs left, either. Where am I?"

"You're in the Second Battalion, Tenth," I said and tossed Lauterbach's rifle back. I told the guy to slide in alongside me. He was pretty jumpy and kept talking about the Jap bayonet attack, but it was nice to have company with a guy who owned a rifle. As it happened, no more Japs came through the gap and at daybreak some reserve troops moved up and took over the foxholes. We went back the CP and began to contact our batteries for artillery fire. And I finally found a rifle.

Dog battery had three guns functional. Easy had one or two. Fox Battery, my old outfit, had been hit bad and was still trying to get organized. I slipped out of the CP and zigzagged to the Fox Battery position to assess their condition. They were trying to get guns and gun crews functional after getting almost totally knocked out during the night.

I ran into Joe Zander smoking a cigarette and noticed he had an extra stripe and was now a staff sergeant. Zander was an old reservist, a hard case with that penetrating stare of a professional warrior who had seen more than he probably wanted to. He had a line on F Battery casualties. First Sergeant Ben Garr had been killed by a hunk of shrapnel that hit him in the forehead. My old friend Roy Auer was dead, along with a bunch of others.

"Auer volunteered to go on a stretcher detail and bring out some guys from a patrol that got ambushed and were down in the swamp," Zander said, matter-of-factly. "Coming back with a casualty on a stretcher, they ran into one of our own machine guns and got cut down."

"Our own gun?"

"Yeah. It was a mix-up in the dark. The kid on the gun was a green replacement, spooked out of his gourd. The first burst went high and missed them. Auer yelled they were Americans, but the kid didn't hear. The second burst caught Roy right in the chest. But the guy on the stretcher didn't get hit. We got him out."

I had enough bad news for now. I shagged back to the Battalion CP and dropped into the pit. Roy Auer. Along with the rows of white crosses when they got the cemetery built on Saipan, there would several markers with the Star of David and one would belong to Roy.

Chapter 18
A Very Bad Day

There is something about sunrise on a battlefield that brings a fervid sense of hope to those who are around to see it. Not only is there a feeling of relief at being alive but also a sense of surprise. In war's carnage, a person adjusts to the idea that time may be running out, that getting hit may be inevitable. With daylight there is also a sense of curiosity to determine what happened during the hours of darkness when chaos ruled.

The coconut grove where our battalion command post was originally set up no longer existed as a coconut grove. The first thing apparent, as daylight arrived, was the scene now looked almost exactly like old photos of the French battlefields in World War I. There were a few torn and scarred tree trunks standing, but most of it was a scene of stubs, stumps, broken machines and earth that had been blown up and turned over again and again. That there were people coming out of holes in this rubble to look around was a miracle in itself.

"Hey, Eddie!

"Mike!"

"I see you made it."

"Just about."

Meeting after a wild night of warfare was like greeting old friends after a long period of separation. Also it was time to catch up on who was hit during the night, who was evacuated, who was dead. It was time to dine on a box of K-Rations, find fresh water and smoke a cigarette. Time to visit the latrine. Bodily functions do not cease just because there is a war on. Sometimes one needs to urinate or defecate in the middle of an artillery barrage or firefight and there is always a good chance of getting shot when engaging in such activity. It is possible to dig a small excavation in the side of a foxhole in which to urinate, and then cover with dirt. But taking a poop under fire is a different matter. Plenty of soldiers have been hit with their hands full of toilet paper. It's just one of those problems that is not discussed in polite company by most military historians.

And after filling a canteen with water, taking care of problems involving elimination and getting something to eat, it is time to buckle down for another day of war, which is ever present.

The persistent Japanese artillery did not allow for any long period of quiet contemplation. As soon as their observers could get fire missions established and shells brought up from supply dumps, they opened up again, partially to get even for the previous night's defeat. After attacking our lines during the night with tanks and massed infantry, the survivors of decimated Jap units vanished into the hills, caves, woods and swamps to set up defenses against the coming counter-attack by our forces. They couldn't push us off their island and they knew we were coming after them.

All of the Second Division artillery units were ashore and operating now. In addition to the 75mm peashooters of the First and Second Battalions, the 105 howitzers of the Third and Fourth

Battalions were now firing. These were key support for the Marines who would be charging across the swamps, through the trees and up the hills in the coming attack. Back in the edge of some still-standing woods near the beach, mobile guns were waiting to move out along with teams of Sherman tanks. Some of the tank teams consisted of two Sherman's and a U.S. Grant tank in the middle. The Grant was lighter but was equipped with a flame thrower that hurled a stream of fire over a hundred yards, a devastating weapon used against tough defenses such as tunnels in rock. In spite of the intense Japanese artillery fire, a steady flood of men, equipment and supplies had come ashore at night and loads of wounded had gone to the hospital ships anchored off shore.

The Japs knew we were getting organized for the assault. To keep our attack off balance and disrupted, enemy big guns opened up again, first with a few shells and then with a steady crescendo of fire. Much of this was aimed a knocking out our artillery units which were causing havoc among the Jap defenders.

It came and went in waves. The Japs would blanket one area with shellfire, then move to another. We knew little brown men hidden in the hills above were watching our every move with powerful field glasses, nodding with grim satisfaction when they saw our artillery pieces knocked out of action, pinpointing those still operating for the next round. We had a few advantages they lacked: For one, we owned the air. From time to time we called on carrier aircraft to come in and wallop the Jap guns operating from the hills. When Jap batteries got particularly troublesome and our ground observers could spot their positions, we called out to the fleet and either destroyers or cruisers would come in and unload. Naval shells have high velocity and low trajectory. We could hear the guns go off on board ship and then the shells would screech overhead and explode on the hillsides. They went over so low you had the feeling that if you stood up, one might take your helmet off.

By mid-morning we were getting raked over pretty well again. Calls of "Corpsman! Corpsman!" increased as a number of people were being hit. Stretcher-bearers were bringing wounded to the aid station, those who could not get there on their own. I was lying on my back in the Command Post watching puffs of white cumulus clouds drifting over when a Jap shell hit one of the few remaining coconut trees standing just a few yards from my fox hole. I heard the howl of the incoming projectile, then the shell exploded in a burst of smoke and flame directly overhead. At the same time, I felt a sudden impact when something hit like a fist to my stomach followed by a burning sensation from hot metal. After the shock, the first thought was: " I'm hit!" But I could still move my arms and legs. Instinctively I clapped both hands over my gut and skidded from my foxhole headfirst into the first aid pit. The blood-spattered battalion doctor and corpsmen were working frantically on a half dozen badly banged up Marines.

One weary corpsman glanced up from his labors, wiped his bloody hands on his dungarees "Where you hit?"

"In the gut," I said as evenly as I could.

He muttered something profane, stepped over and knelt down. Without looking, I pulled my hands away from my middle. He snorted. "It's not life-threatening."

I ventured a look. The shell fragment had come at an angle, had cut through the skin and traveled horizontally along an abdominal muscle to a place below and under the skin to the left of my belly button. Maybe it had gone through part of the coconut tree first, lessening its impact. The corpsman took a scalpel, made a small incision and flipped out the piece of hot metal. He dumped some sulfa on the cut and slapped a bandage over it.

"You're O.K." He wiped his hands. "You want me to write it up?"

I felt embarrassed with my dingy little cut when the pit was full of people with broken bones and massive gashes. Even to consider a write-up for a Purple Heart was embarrassing. "Forget it," I said, scrambling to my feet. "The way things are going, I'll be back with a real one."

I crawled out and slid into the fire control pit. Communications had been restored. I moved to the switchboard and put on a head set. Somebody said: "We heard you got hit."

"Almost missed," I answered.

With what artillery pieces the battalion could muster, we began firing as targets were called in. Lt. Ormond, at the Forward OP, between missions asked: "Did any of you guys see Boyd back there?" Boyd was one of several American Indians in Headquarters Company. He was a Dakota, I think. He was a tough, wiry guy and a dead shot with a rifle. I told Lt. Ormond we hadn't seen Boyd around the area. "Isn't he supposed to be with you at the OP?" I asked.

"Yeah," said Lt. Ormond. "But he turned up missing last night during a fire mission. He didn't get hit and he isn't around here. I think he deserted under fire and I want him on report."

I couldn't believe Boyd deserted. More likely, I thought, he took a shell dead center and vanished in puff of blood and rags. Another candidate for "Tomb of the Unknown Soldier."

Over the switchboard, our outpost observers were giving us a play-by-play on the Marine attack. Some units of the Second, Sixth and Eighth Regiments were on the move storming across the swamps, through the cedar brush and into the hills. On our left, men and tanks were rolling toward the city of Garapan. The Japs were contesting every inch of the way. Around noon, our Battalion Commander, Colonel Shell was out walking around, checking the unit, showing his contempt for Jap gunners. He was absolutely fearless, but some of us worried that his walking around would draw fire from enemy observers in the hills. We were getting reports on the advancing troops and attempted to bring fire on Jap strong points, machinegun nests or whatever held up the advance. The Colonel was standing by one of our radio Jeeps along with Paul Ryan, a member of my squad, and the Jeep driver who was seated at the wheel. Somehow a Jap mortar crew had penetrated our defenses and were set up in a clump of brush a few hundred yards away. We heard the faint "foomp!" as the mortars left the tubes but assumed they were ours until they exploded. Two hit the Jeep with ear-shattering detonations, followed by several more nearby. When the smoke and dust cleared, we heard the Colonel calling: "Corpsman! Corpsman!" I looked over the rim of the command post to see Col. Shell and Ryan both flat on the ground, the Jeep driver slumped against the steering wheel. More mortars came in while several of us slid out and dragged the Colonel, Ryan and the driver into the first aid pit. All three were a mess. The Jeep driver had a big hole in his upper leg where the brake pedal had been blown right through it. A corpsman gave him a morphine shot while the doctor stopped the bleeding and taped on a compress.

Ryan's eyes were jumping with pain. He had taken a number of mortar fragments in his right leg but didn't seem go have any broken bones. The Colonel was really torn up. A piece of his upper leg bone was gone. He was a muscular guy and his knee had jerked up several inches toward his hip. He was bleeding badly from the face, arms and chest. He didn't look good, but his voice was strong. "Houston!" he yelled. "Houston!"

Major Kenneth Houston, our battalion exec officer and second in command, slid in the pit alongside Colonel Shell as the doctor and the corpsmen were strapping the Colonel to a wire stretcher to immobilize his shattered leg. Shell lay on his back with blood leaking out of him in a dozen places, barking operational orders for the next two days at Houston. Houston bent over, repeating the orders.

One of our radiomen had called the beach and requested a halftrack be sent to pick up the Colonel, Ryan and the Jeep driver. There were several armored halftracks in the same patch of jumbled and shattered woods where the burned-out Jap tanks were sitting. The radioman yelled at us: "The halftrack guys say they aren't about to come out in the open where we are, but if we can get our wounded to the woods, they will get them to the beach!"

First Sergeant Bittick was swearing up his usual storm, threatening to kill the halftrack drivers. I figured maybe they were right. If they came out in the open and got blown up, nobody would be going anywhere.

The doctor had two volunteers with the stretcher holding Colonel Shell, who was now shot full of morphine, and two more manning a stretcher with the Jeep driver. "When we get a lull," the doctor said. "Run these people to the woods. Get them out of here before they get hit again."

I poked Paul Ryan. "If I get under your right shoulder, do you think you can make it to the halftracks?"

Paul nodded, sweat cutting lines down the dirt on his face.

The shelling let up and the stretcher-bearers were on their feet, out of the aid pit and running for the woods. "Let's go!" I yelled at Paul.

I got under his right shoulder and he hobbled along groaning, with the weight on his good left leg, as we started for the woods. About halfway there, the Jap mortar crew opened up again and the stretcher-bearers lit out like the wind. With the first bang, Paul let out a yell and bolted for the woods, bad leg and all. He took off so fast I landed face first in the dirt and looked up in time to see him sprint to safety among the trees. In spite of the whole mess I had to laugh at how fast Paul ran when his survival was at stake, banged up leg and all. Ryan, Shell and the driver all made it. Shell was seen months later in San Diego limping around with a cane. Ryan got most of the tin removed from his leg and three weeks later was back with our outfit although small pieces of metal kept showing up under the skin on his leg and had to be cut out. The Jeep driver got a trip home.

His war was over but he was alive.

By afternoon, things had calmed down a little and Bittick came over to the CP. "Cary, on your feet. We've gotta go down to the beach and pick up a bunch of replacements."

In a way, we were glad to get the replacements. It seemed like about half the battalion had been knocked out of action. On the other hand, these would be raw recruits, green and untrained in battle. We had our work cut out.

Bittick and I zig-zagged toward the beach, dropping into shell holes when we heard incoming ordnance. We sprinted across the concrete air strip, noting the wrecked observation planes. In fox holes just on the other side of the strip, were some guys who didn't look exactly like Marines. For one thing, they looked lot older.

"What outfit?" Bittick asked.

"Sea Bees," one guy answered.

"Sea Bees? Whatta you guys doing dug in here? You're supposed to be building docks and stuff on the beach."

"When the Japs broke through the lines the other night, they had us come up and plug the hole." one Sea Bee said.

"Yeah," another guy answered. "Some Marine captain came down to the beach and said if we didn't come up and help out, the Japs would be down on the beach with us...so we moved up."

Bittick laughed and we kept walking. On the beach we found the troop depot where the new Marines were coming ashore. Bittick located the officer in charge and then got the roster of replacements assigned to the Second Battalion, about 18 of them. It was a shock to see how young they looked. Just kids. Their faces reflected the usual mixture of worry, curiosity, pride and determination. And we found out something else. Some of them were draftees, the first we had seen up to now. All the Marines we knew had been volunteers - hard cases, shooters, street fighters, didn't-give-a-damn brawlers looking for trouble, men who knew the risks and offered to take them. A few were fresh out of prison. They had a rule in California that men serving, say, a one-to-four sentence for robbery, could sign up and serve their time in the Marine Corps and come out with their records wiped clean. We knew who some of these were and we didn't ask questions. We also had a few hard cases from Mexico who signed up with the understanding that if they made it through, they would become U.S. citizens.

But these new troops, the draftees, had the luck or lack thereof to be assigned to the Marine Corps where life was chancy, at best. I didn't even want to think about it.

We formed the replacements into a single file. Bittick walked down the row, fingering his Colt .45, looking every man in the in the eyes, then stepped back. "You will each be assigned to one old guy until you learn your trade," he barked. "If you stick with him and pay attention, you may survive! You do what he does. If he ducks, you duck. If he runs, you run. You will not waste your time thinking of your own safety. You simply react. We have a mission and that is to kill all the goddam enemy we can find. You will focus at all times on the mission. Got it? O.K! Move out!"

We threaded our way back through whatever cover we could find, but for some reason, the Jap artillery had let up. We jogged across the scarred up air strip, then hiked past the battalion of burned out Jap tanks. All heads turned and eyed the wreckage. "Jap tank attack," Bittick explained laconically. "Good fight. Every damn one of 'em got killed."

We pulled up at the Battalion CP where officers from the three batteries were on hand to get whatever replacements they could. They didn't totally fill all the gaps in the ranks, but they were a start. Bittick looked at the six assigned to Battalion Headquarters and grumbled toward me: "Do you think any of these guys will be alive next week?"

"For cripes sake, Bittick, will you shut up?" I growled.

165

"These kids are scared out of their pants already." Bittick just laughed. He was an extremely tough Marine, a fearless leader, but sometimes had a problem with common sense.

I adopted one 18 year-old replacement, an Italian kid from Chicago by the name of Frank Cirricione. "Look, Frank," I said. "I am going to give you a crash course in survival. You pay attention, you hear? I am going to see that your parents get their kid back." Frank nodded and grinned broadly. He wasn't afraid. He may have been a draftee, but he was going to be a good Marine.

There was a piece of funny news swept through the ranks a couple of days later: "Hey, you hear what ol' Howlin' Mad Smith did? The word is that he fired the Army general and shipped him home!"

"The hell!"

There had been a smoldering dispute going on with the Second Marine Division, the Fourth Marine Division and the Army 27th Division. The Fourth was driving up the east coast and we in the Second were strung out up the west coast. The 27th was in between and ran into a Japanese strong point that turned out to be a clinker. They lost some men and their attack bogged down. In the meantime the Second and Fourth were pushing ahead which made the line loop back in the shape of a "U" with Japs in the middle where they could attack our flanks. Marine General Holland Smith, overall ground commander of the invasion, told Army General Ralph Smith to get his troops moving and wipe out that "U" loop. The Army General Smith said he wanted artillery, tanks and air support. The Marine Smith said he would get what everybody got, which was not much, but get going. The 27th didn't move.

Old Howlin' Mad called in the Army General, relieved him of his command, put him on a plane and shipped him to Hawaii. There was an Associated Press reporter covering the invasion and when his story hit the newspapers in the states, it created

166

quite a stir. Some of the Army brass plus some Washington politicians wanted to hang Howlin' Mad by his neck, but we thought his action was appropriate. The Army sent General Sanderford Jarman to take over and right after that the 27th got moving, caught up with the Second and Fourth and straightened out the line. The attack continued with everybody moving ahead.

While the stalemate was going on, Carl Houston and I made a sashay down to where our people were busy taking the city of Garapan. The first Marines we ran into were coming up the street with pockets full of Japanese money. "Our bazooka guy blew the door off the bank vault," one Marine announced. "There's money all over the place."

Carl and I ran for the bank, a big stone structure that had withstood the Naval bombardment even though about everything else around it was flattened. We headed for the vault where a dozen Marines were buy picking over stacks of money and we each got a big roll of bills we secured with thick rubber bands. These were 5,000 and 10,000 yen notes with pictures of the Japanese emperor on the front. It was island money, invasion money, and wasn't really worth anything, but Carl and I returned to Headquarters as Japanese millionaires.

But before we headed back, we went up Garapan's main street a little way to see how that part of the war was going. Several grimy Marines were sitting in the shade behind the rubble of an office building, smoking cigarettes and looking pretty depressed.

"Tough day?" Carl inquired.

"Rotten war," one Marine grumbled. "Ain't worth fightin'."

"Lose a lot of friends?" we asked.

"Nah, nothin' like that. We lost the brewery."

Carl eyed the guys. "The brewery?"

"Yeah," one Marine flipped his cigarette butt into the rubble. "We been fightin' for two days to capture the Jap brewery...a big one on the edge of town. We were downwind from the brewery and we could smell the beer which gave us a lot of incentive, only the Japs weren't going to give it up easy."

Another Marine got in on the conversation: "Yeah. We were workin' on the problem, moving up through the rubble; taking out a Nip here, a Nip there. We picked up casualties in the process. Somebody at headquarters figured we had too many getting hit, so they ordered us to drop back while the Navy shelled the place and blew it flat." The Marine shook his head. "Broke every damn bottle in there. The wind blew the smell over us and it was awful. Enough to make you wanna quit fightin' this crummy war!"

Carl and I agreed it was a crummy war. I noticed one of the guys had a tank on his back. "You a regular flame thrower operator?"

"Yeah, since the landing."

"You're lucky to be still walking around," I observed. "The whole Jap army likes to shoot at the flamethrower operators …they hate you guys."

"Yeah. They say the average flamethrower operator has about three hours to live in combat," the Marine laughed. "I'm running way ahead on overtime."

"The odds are not good," I agreed. "I think I'd look for other work."

"Yeah." The guy laughed again and ran his hand lightly over the metal flamethrower nozzle. "But, geez, I love this tool!"

To each his own. Houston and I wished the three guys well and headed back to our position. The Marine/Army advance had overrun a lot of the Jap artillery units in the hills and we were no longer getting hammered by big stuff. There was just a stray shell rolling in every 20 minutes or so from somewhere on the other side of Garapan. The Japs just wanted to remind us that the war wasn't over yet.

Chapter 19
It Doesn't Get Any Worse

The trucks started coming in the morning and unloading in the blown-out area behind our position. We had been in the same place for several days, ready to move out, but with no orders to move. The whole front was stagnant due to the flap with the Army 27th Division, which was also not moving. The thing was, we were supposed to be a couple of miles farther north, but because the Army wasn't moving, the Second Division couldn't move. Somebody in division supply had a timetable, which had nothing to do with the war. The timetable said on D-plus-6, bring in more ammunition and stack it up in a rear area out of combat. The only problem there was no rear area out of combat.

Out of curiosity, Sgt. Englehardt and I decided to go take a look. I motioned to Pvt. Cirricione to come along. The trucks were unloading tons of stuff - 75mm shells, 105mm shells, 155 shells, land mines, small arms ammo and crate after crate of pyrotechnics and dynamite. Row upon row, stack upon stack.

This was scary stuff right next to our position and within a rifle shot of the front lines. The only non-scary thing was that some of the shell boxes were stenciled as coming from the federal ordnance factory at Joliet, Illinois, my hometown. In the fall before the war had started, I had a job as a timekeeper with a construction crew building that factory. I was earning money to go back and finish college when the Japs hit Pearl Harbor. Just about everybody I knew left for the war but here were all these crates of shells from my home town. It was a small world.

Englehardt, Cirricione and I went back to where the First Sergeant was sitting by his foxhole and asked if he knew what was going on behind us.

"Yeah, they're bringing in supplies." Bittick said.

"Explosives," Englehardt pointed out. "Ammo, artillery shells, flares, dynamite, mines, all piled up together."

Bittick blinked. "All that stuff together?"

"Yeah. One shell in there and the whole dump goes off like Fourth of July."

Bittick whistled, got up and said he was going over for a look. We went with him. He stared at the stuff, eyed the labels on the boxes, shook his head and swore softly. "I gotta tell the skipper about this," he said, indicating that Captain Finn ought to know that we were sitting on the edge of a very explosive pile.

In a couple of minutes, we saw Bittick and Captain Finn go over for a look. They came back with Finn shaking his head in disbelief. The Captain slid into the CP and grabbed a field phone. He got through to Regimental Headquarters and inquired as to just who the hell authorized piling all that stuff together in our backyard. He got pretty angry but it was apparent he couldn't find anyone who could understand the situation.

In the meantime, more and more trucks came in and unloaded. The dump was now 75 yards long and 40 yards wide. The crates were stacked as high as a man could reach. There hadn't been much Jap shelling for a half-day, but the Japs obviously knew where we were and could lob stuff in on us at any time. One shell in that pile of explosives and it might blow the island in half.

Bittick was still swearing up a storm about how somebody in supply was totally stupid. "Hey, Bittick," I said. "If the Division insists on piling that stuff there, why don't we move the battalion? There're no Japs directly in front of us now. The Second Regiment has cleared them out almost to Garapan. We could move a half mile north and get away from this stuff."

"The Captain already thought of that, but we didn't get any orders to move."

"Does anybody on this island have any idea how dangerous this pile of staff is sitting out here?"

"Don't tell me," Bittick said. "I am not in charge. Anyway, the word is, we'll be moving out tomorrow."

"What's wrong with today."

"The orders are for tomorrow. Besides, it is a good location for a dump."

"How's that?"

"They are laying out the Second Division Cemetery on the other side. If the dump blows up, they won't have far to drag us to bury us."

"Geez, Bittick," I said. "You are a bundle of joy."

Somebody brought us several cases of K Rations and we sat down by our foxholes to eat supper. One of the corporals came over with a canteen. "Want a slug of lime juice?

"Where'd you get the lime juice?"

"From limes. We found a tree with limes and squeezed out some."

I took a hefty slug and it was pretty good. The corporal took his canteen back and walked away. "Hey, where did you find the lime tree?" I yelled after him. He looked back and laughed. He wasn't letting his secret out.

The trucks quit running to the dump as it started to get dark. Somebody had posted several guards around the edges, but I couldn't see how that was going to help if the Japs shelled us. Before dark, I told Cirricione that we would enlarge our foxholes and dig a little deeper. "I don't like the powder keg next door," I said. "If that sucker goes off, it will level everything around here."

Frank nodded and began digging.

It was a hot night and nobody was sleeping much. Somewhere in the dark nearby we heard a sentry yell out: "Halt! Who goes there?"

This was followed by another yell, a rifle shot and a then couple of grenades went off. The first box of dynamite blew up with a loud bang. Whoever the infiltrator was, he knew his target. This was followed by a pause and we could see the orange glow of a fire starting. Then a bunch of 105 shells started popping, sending projectiles crashing into the woods...

At this point, the battalion supply officer, Captain Nolan, came racing up yelling: "Everybody out! Everybody out! Grab your shovels and follow me. We've gotta put this fire out!"

By the sputtering light of the fire, we could see few guys climbing out of their foxholes with their shovels. Frank Cirricione started to get up and I grabbed his shirt and shoved him back. "Stay put!" I hissed. "This whole damn thing is gonna blow."

Against the glow of the growing, popping fire, the first bunch of volunteers could be seen tossing sand on the burning ammo. They might just as well have been spitting into a volcano. Captain Nolan came running back yelling for more volunteers when the whole works went up. The crash must have been heard in downtown Tokyo. The dump became a thundering inferno with shells exploding and belts of 50-caliber machine gun ammo going off like strings of huge firecrackers. All we could do was hug the shaking ground, pray and duck as shells of all sizes whizzed and howled through the air. The explosions con-

172

tinued for two terrifying hours then simmered down to an ordinary fire with just an occasional crash of something going off. As daylight began to arrive from the east, the explosions quit. The fires had diminished to clouds of white smoke saturated with the smell of burned gunpowder. There was nothing more to blow up. We crept out of our holes cautiously for a look. Outside of a few burning piles of junk, the dump was gone. Vanished. Scattered about like bundles of charred rags were the bodies of a dozen of our people on the edge of where the dump once stood. A dozen dead. Included was a good friend, Joe Henger. Killed by the blast.

Some guys were rolling over the dead to identify them. "I don't see Captain Nolan here," one Marine muttered.

"Hell, he wasn't in the fire," was the bitter retort. "He got those guys to go in with their shovels and he ran back to get more volunteers. That dummy was a hundred yards away when it blew up."

I went back to the foxhole to check on Cirricione. "Frank!" I called. He was hunched up in his hole and didn't move. I grabbed him by the shoulder and rolled him over. His face was a mass of blood. "Oh migod!" I thought. Some of the junk hit him in the head and killed him!"

About then, he groaned and sat up, wiping a hand through the blood and staring at it. I was relieved to see he wasn't dead, but couldn't tell exactly how bad his injuries were. I yelled for a corpsman who came over and wiped off the blood. What had happened was, when the dump blew, a bunch of huge disc-shaped land mines went flying through the air and one smacked Cirricione, broke the bridge of his nose, cut his face and knocked him cold; but outside of that he was O.K. The corpsman cleaned up his face and taped his nose. "We'll have the doctor take a look as soon as he gets a chance."

Cirricione sat up on the side of the foxhole, looking around sort of dopey, but grinning. I knew he was glad just to be alive.

"Frank," I said." I think you are gonna make it O.K. Last night they called your number and you got missed. You'll probably make it fine from here on."

While talking to some of the other guys, we pieced together what probably happened. While we were worried about Jap artillery, that's not what got the dump. Apparently, several Japs with grenades infiltrated during the night. The dump had been spotted from the hills and they knew exactly what they were looking for. Our sentry either saw or heard one of the Japs and challenged him. Then he took a shot at him; but one of the Japs threw a grenade into the dump and up it went.

There was a lot of talk around the command post about what a brave guy Captain Nolan was to lead the charge into the ammo fire. The word was that they were going to write him up for a Silver Star. The facts were, he may have been brave, but what he did was stupid. And he was still alive and 12 good men were dead for no good reason.

And then, about 10 o'clock, orders came through for us to move the battalion a half mile north. We lost 12 buddies because the order came a day late. When we were loading up the trucks and jeeps to move, Frank came over and offered a cigarette.

"Sarge," he said. "I just wanted to say thanks for holding me down last night. I could've gone up in smoke with those other guys."

"You're a gutsy guy, Frank," I pointed out. "But along with guts, you've got to stay alert and keep thinking if you want to get through this war."

He nodded and I helped myself to another one of his cigarettes.

Chapter 20
Moving to the Suburbs

The day after the dump blew up, we loaded into 3/4 ton trucks and jeeps, moving the whole battalion north a mile and setting up on a plateau overlooking a stretch of beach by the City of Garapan. The surf was rolling over the outer reef, churning the water to a milky blue. On the outside of the reef, by contrast, the Pacific Ocean stretched a deep ultramarine blue to the horizon. If it hadn't been for the occasional Jap shell and the ever-present stink of dead bodies, it would have been pleasant.

We hadn't gotten the Battalion Command Post set up when Lieutenant Randall began getting really excited. Randall was a replacement, new to the battalion. He let it be known that he had graduated at the top of his class from the Marine Artillery School. Indeed, he loved to talk about artillery theory and the use of survey data for pinpoint accuracy. Nobody paid much attention to him until we got on the plateau overlooking the sea. "There it is!" he yelled in exultation. "The classic set up!"

He pointed to bare ridge a quarter mile east and a sandy point on the beach below sticking out into the ocean. "We can set up a survey pole on the ridge, another down on the point. Perfect triangulation! We can hit anything on the map. We can pinpoint every Jap position right from here and blow it away!"

Nobody else was that enthusiastic about some textbook method of removing the enemy, but Randall babbled on. Next, he sent a private scrambling through the brush to install a red-and-white survey pole on the ridge and then sent PFC Rooney with another pole to stick out on the sandy point. In the meantime, Randall set up a transit on a tri-pod so he could line in on the poles with accuracy.

We watched idly as Rooney went loping downhill to the beach and then up along shore toward the point. He was just a small, distant figure, but we could see him very clearly running along the sand. Suddenly, we saw him stop, hurl the pole into the sea and come sprinting back down the beach. Eventually, he made it up the hill, through the brush and back to our position. Randall was livid. He grabbed Rooney by he shirt and yelled in his face: "You disobeyed an order! Whatta you mean by throwing that survey pole in the water and running back up here?"

Rooney, wild-eyed and sweating, managed to gasp: "We don't own that point, sir. There's nobody down there except Japanese."

Captain Finn glanced over. "What happened, son?"

"I was running up the beach with the pole like the lieutenant said," Rooney gulped. "Ran past a lot of Marines who were digging trenches and all of a sudden I was in with some other guys who were digging trenches only they were Japanese!"

Everybody stopped whatever they were doing to listen in. "They must have been construction workers or something because they didn't have any weapons. At least, none of them shot at me as I ran out of there."

"Why did you throw away that survey pole?" Lieutenant

Randall persisted.

"It was slowing me down," noted Rooney.

"That's Marine Corps property...." Randall started to say but Captain Finn broke in: "For cripes sake, Randall, shut up! The kid could've gotten killed."

Randall climbed into the CP pit and sat down. His face was red and he was embarrassed. And he should have been.

There was not a whole lot going on. The Japs had moved back to a line that led up a ridge from just east of Garapan to the peak of 1,500-foot Mount Topotcho, the highest point on the island. A few stray shells came whistling in, but did little damage. On top of outbreaks of malaria, experienced periodically by the Guadalcanal veterans, there was another mosquito-carried disease on Saipan called dengue fever. It acted much the same way with chills and high fever, usually with vomiting and fierce headaches. We had a couple of guys who had all that and dysentery, too. A couple of real messes, who lay in their foxholes, sweated, moaned, shook and crawled out to poop. Bittick came over and said for me to get a stretcher jeep and transport the two sickest ones to the hospital. The division medical center was located in the old Saipan radio station on the outskirts of Garapan.

The pair of dengue fever victims from Headquarters Company was in bad shape but not nearly as bad off as the casualty from Fox Battery who was in a Jeep ahead of us. He was a replacement, probably 17 years old, and he had taken a metal shell hunk through the middle of his back. They had him lying face down on a stretcher hung on a rack inside the Jeep. As we started down the hill toward the hospital, both Jeeps swayed back and forth and the wounded guy rolled from side to side. It looked like there wasn't much holding him together below his rib cage. A corpsman was riding in the back of the jeep to hold the plasma bottle and make sure the tubes didn't get pulled out of the guy. One of our sick guys had gotten out of the stretcher, slumped in the front seat of my Jeep holding onto the windshield. The other guy lay in the back, hunched over. The road was full of ruts and rocks. It was a hard ride, but it was the only way we could do it.

We drove as carefully as we could down to the radio station, trying not to jostle the sick and the wounded guy. My patients managed to stumble into the admitting desk on their own. The corpsman and I carried the stretcher with the shot-up Marine into the operating room, which held a bloody collection of human wreckage. Somewhere up in the hills a lot of war was going on and they were bringing in dozens of torn up Marines for the doctors and nurses to work on. A nurse pointed to a table where we laid the stretcher with our guy. As we prepared to leave, the wounded Marine from Fox Battery caught my eye and muttered, "How's it look?"

Migod. He was almost cut in half. I managed somehow to force a grin and give the kid a "thumbs up." His eyes were jumping with pain, but he grinned back. He looked like he had maybe an hour or two. I hoped they'd keep him full of morphine until he quit breathing. But then, you never knew. The medical people saved a lot of guys who looked like they wouldn't last another hour. We had a saying which may or may not have been right, but it was: "If they can get you to the hospital, you're gonna live."

The operating room was a churning mess. Doctors were working at top speed, moving from patient to patient and the nurses were running back and forth with instruments, bandages and medications. Neither the doctors nor nurses looked like they'd had any sleep for a week and they probably hadn't. Orderlies with bags moved around collecting arms, legs and other bits of human anatomy. It was pretty grim stuff and I didn't stick around very long.

On the far side of the hospital there was a dining tent with a long chow line but I didn't feel much like eating. Still I stopped and thought about it. They were serving real food to the patients who could walk. One guy standing in line on crutches looked at

178

me and looked away, then looked back and stared hard. I recognized him from somewhere. Maybe boot camp, I thought. He pulled out of the line and limped over to where I was standing. "Cary?" he asked.

"Yeah, I'm Cary. I know you from somewhere"

"I'm Lyons. Hamilton Lyons. From back home."

"Ham Lyons! Migod!" He had grown a black beard and looked a lot older than the high school kid who lived two blocks away in my hometown. "Geez, Lyons," I pointed at the crutches. "What happened to you?"

"Got hit with a Jap mortar, first day." He stuck out a bandaged left leg for me to see. "I been here ever since while they keep digging scrap iron outta my leg."

"You're the first guy I've seen from back home in three years, Lyons. What outfit are you in?"

"Second regiment. I was on Tarawa."

"The Second got chewed up pretty bad there," I noted.

"Yeah. I got hit there the first day, too. Was ashore about two hours, went over the beach wall and got nailed going after a machine gun in a pillbox. He hit me in the right leg and I rolled up to the pillbox, just below the gun port. The Jap couldn't tip the machine gun muzzle low enough to finish me off." He laughed at the thought. "I laid just below that machine gun muzzle for over an hour until one of our guys threw a grenade in the pillbox and checked him off. I had three hours on Tarawa and four hours here on Saipan. I've had two landings and two purple hearts for seven hours of combat."

We both laughed out loud. "Hey, they got roast beef for lunch," Lyons said. "Real stuff. Grab a tray and let's eat!"

We got into the chow line, loaded our trays and found a couple seats. The food was good. Even had pie for dessert. Lyons and I compared notes. Since I had left home over a year before Lyons, he filled me in on what had happened around town up until he shipped out. We kidded at length about some of the good-looking girls we knew in school. Lyons was a handsome kid. Even when he was in high school the younger college women went nuts over him and he enjoyed it all. But he decided he wanted to go fight and he signed up for the Marines after high school graduation and left.

Lyons' dad had died when he was little kid and his mother raised him. It was not any easy job during the Depression, but somehow they made it. We talked about the old neighborhood, the kids we grew up with, and the stuff we did. First thing, it was suppertime. I figured what the heck; just as well get two good meals before going back up on the plateau. So we went to supper. Lyons was really hurting but he gimped along on the crutches. After supper we went back to the hospital tent which housed about 40 casualties and talked into dark.

"Condition red!"

A corpsman with a flashlight came rushing through, rousting patients out. "Air raid! Take cover! Condition red! Move out to a shelter!"

Ham didn't feel like walking so we both just sat there, smoking and talking some more. Three Jap bombers came droning in high from somewhere, looking for the airfield. Searchlights were probing all over the sky and the antiaircraft guns began pumping away.

The corpsman came running back to check the tent once more, saw us and yelled: "You better get to a shelter trench! The Jap's are here!"

"How do you know they won't drop a bomb in the shelter trench," Lyons yelled back.

The corpsman swore at us and left. We stayed put and watched the air show with Jap bombers appearing like tiny silver model airplanes overhead in the searchlight beams, puffs of ack-ack all around them.

All of a sudden Lyons groaned in a strained voice: "I gotta go."

Along with the iron in his leg, he also had an acute case of the drizzlies - amoebic dysentery. This was serious. Lyons got up on his crutches and I helped him limp out of the tent into the night. "There's a latrine right over there somewhere," Lyons aimed a crutch off into the dark. We moved that way, Lyons hobbling and moaning with every step. Visibility was bad, especially trying to see anything against the dark ground. When we finally spotted a trench, Lyons dropped his pants and straddled the gap. Right about then a tense voice called up from the dark trench below:

"Lookout! Lookout! This ain't no latrine! This is an air raid trench!"

It was too late. Lyons had already cut loose. He hastily wiped with a fistful of toilet paper, pulled up his pants and we headed back to the tent. We never knew what happened to whoever was in that slit trench. Lyons said the guy probably wished he had been hit by one of the Jap bombers.

Just as it was getting toward daylight, I hopped in the Jeep; and rumbled back up to the battalion command post. "Where in hell you been?" Bittick yelled as I pulled in.

"I took three guys to the hospital. One of them was a kid I knew from Fox Battery. He was shot up pretty bad and I hung around to see if he was going to make it," I lied.

"Did they pull him through?"

"Geez, I dunno. The last I saw of him he was still alive." That part, at least, was the truth. I didn't feel too bad.

Chapter 21
The Last Gasp on Saipan

Taking Mt. Tapotchau was the clincher for Saipan. Once the Marine Second, Marine Fourth and Army 27th divisions took the heights, we were above the enemy, looking down on them like they had been looking down on us from the assault on the beachhead, across the swamps and on our bloody ascent upward. From the crest of Tapotchau and the ridges on both sides, we could not only see the far end of the island, but below and to our left we could see the smooth sand beaches, the huge fleet of Navy PBY flying boats and swimmers. With field glasses we could make out flight crews diving off the seaplanes, lucky sailors and a few Navy nurses cooling off in the surf. It had an appearance of unreality. Down below, there was no war, just blue water, white sand and palm trees. Up on the crest, it was rock, wet clay, trees, brush, heat, explosions, tracers, imminent death and stink. Two weeks of destruction had littered the terrain with Jap and American bodies.

The Second Battalion 10th had been moved up the side of the mountain to a position just a whisker back from the crest where Japanese forward observers could not get a good fix on our guns. We were in a strategic spot to rain death down on the defenders entrenched and largely invisible in the greenery below. Battalion headquarters was situated astride a muddy supply road that zig-zagged its way nearly to the mountaintop. My squad was assigned a sheltered spot behind a sheer rock ledge that afforded excellent protection from Jap counter-artillery fire. We set about digging in for defense against an expected ground assault. We were aware that the cornered enemy was extremely dangerous and would continually probe our defenses for weak spots. We knew they would mount a wild banzai charge if the opportunity arose.

The fight for the top of the mountain had been bitter and vicious. Hundreds of the enemy had been taken down by shellfire, rifle fire, machine gun fire, hand grenades and flame-throwers. Although the dead defenders had been buried as fast as the situation stabilized, there was still a distinct aroma of death permeating the ridge. We had our howitzers in place and fire missions on the way almost as soon as we reached the   crest in the afternoon. I was included in the team directing fire as our forward observers called in targets. Thus, several of us didn't get our foxholes dug until relieved in the evening.

As the sun waned, the air cooled and the breeze off the ocean diminished, the smell of death grew progressively stronger. I became aware, as my foxhole neared completion, that the particular spot I had chosen for my hole, against the cliff, seemed to be smellier than, say, 30 feet away. I began looking around for the source. Eventually, I spotted several muddy fingers protruding from the ground. I dug around them and determined that they were part of a hand. The question naturally arose: Was the hand loose or attached to an arm?

With the entire hand revealed, I reached down, gripped it

184

and gave it a tug. It didn't come loose. I dug a little more and gave it a stronger tug. The smell became more acute. Apparently there was a body on the other end. With the shovel I piled a mound of clay around the hand and erased it from sight. All this time my squad watched intently, aware of the problem but offering no comment. With the hand back underground, the odor lessened somewhat and as darkness moved in, I tidied up the foxhole, tucked a few grenades into a side shelf and adjusted for the night.

We fully expected a Japanese counter attack that night, but it didn't materialize. Sporadic Jap artillery fire crashed along the mountain ridge and mortars whammed in among the rocks, but it was mostly random nuisance fire, nothing like the shelling we had experienced near the beach. Navy ships kept a steady supply of star shells sputtering over the mountain so we could see if the enemy was out in force. It was a relatively quiet night with nothing moving in the darkness. Toward morning, it began to rain a solid downpour that converted our foxholes to pockets of soupy muck. We huddled under our ponchos, trying to keep our weapons dry and simultaneously swatted at squadrons of mosquitoes bent on draining our blood. By daylight, I became aware that the stench that had diminished the night before had now returned in force. It was nearly overpowering.

By first light I immediately spotted the problem: The hand had not only come out of its mud sarcophagus, but part of the Jap's head and shoulder were now protruding. I guessed that during the night, the body had absorbed considerable moisture, swelled up and was climbing out of the ground. Developing a considerable distaste for this turn of events, I got out in the mud with my shovel and piled more clay on the offending cadaver. The clay was soft, wet and malleable which assisted my effort to re-inter the deceased. Naturally, all of this activity drew the attention of my comrades who now felt compelled to offer bits of advice and comment. Corporal Lenox opined that the dead Jap emerging from the mud compared favorably with my mud-spattered appearance. He suggested that the dead man even smelled better. I threatened to smash him with my shovel. He laughed but shut up.

Eventually, I got the exposed parts of the corpse packed with an extra –thick mound of clay and muck, which seemed to solve the problem. Fire missions came in and the day evolved into the usual routine of load, shoot, haul ammo and duck incoming fire. Our forward observers were well above the enemy, in excellent position to direct devastating fire on their defenses. The voices on the radio from our observers were almost gleeful as we poured round after round of high explosives into the palm-studded farmland below. Again, we anticipated a sudden attack that night, but it didn't happen. The enemy was apparently content to wait, slow our advance and watch for an opportunity to strike.

At daybreak, my deceased Japanese adversary was back out of the ground. During the day, the stifling heat apparently dried him up somewhat, but at night he absorbed more moisture, and swelled up, emerging from his mud cover. This was finally too much. In a lather of profanity, I gathered up my pack, poncho and rifle and moved 30 yards along the ridge to dig a new foxhole. This was much to the hilarity of the squad who noted that this was the first time they had ever seen a Marine driven from the field of battle by a dead enemy. I didn't think it was particularly funny, but it was a relief to put some distance between the corpse and myself.

The Army 27th Division, which had fought well at times, but had been the subject of considerable controversy from the start - including removal of their division commander - moved through our position and took over the area in front of us and between us and the shore. Marine units dropped back into reserve positions all along the line except for our battalion and the third battalion of our regiment, a 105-mm howitzer unit that remained in close support of the Army. There is always confusion on a battlefield, but the confusion within the 27th command was of epic dimension. There was a gap between two Army battalions, which did not get repaired before dark. It was exactly what the Japanese were looking for. About midnight, all hell broke loose in front and to our left as several thousand Japanese infantry, the remainder of their tanks, plus what was left of their naval artillery forces and support troops erupted in a massive banzai charge.

Our first inkling of how serious the situation had become occurred when an Army captain came pounding up the hillside in the light of a flare and jumped into our battalion command post where we were operating by flashlight "We were overrun!" he screamed. "We were overrun! Give me a phone! I've got to contact division headquarters!"

Captain Finn was on duty in the CP and he centered his flashlight on the agitated Army captain. "Where is your command?" Finn bellowed.

"Down below! We were overrun! I've got to call Division."

"Damn you, man!" Finn abruptly cut in. "You deserted your men! And where the hell is your weapon?" The captain carried no rifle.

As the Army captain sputtered, Finn yelled at a nearby rifleman: "This officer is under arrest! Don't let him out of here… if he moves, shoot him!" The army captain turned white and his eyes grew even wider with fear.

Finn got on the radio and established contact with our division headquarters who were now aware the Japanese attack was massive and well in progress. Finn got the captain's name and relayed that information to our command, suggesting the Army 27th headquarters be informed of the matter and send someone up to retrieve their hero. Then we buckled down for a long night.

On the flat below us, between our position and the beach, the night was cut up with streams of machine gun tracers and flashes of grenade bursts. Then the machine guns, rifles and 105's of the third battalion began to crash, indicating that the enemy had broken through the Army defenses and were now into the artillery positions and perhaps beyond. The third battalion gunners drew their perimeter tight and fired their cannons point blank at the attackers, finally skip-firing the shells to bounce and explode in front of the attacking enemy no more than a couple hundred yards distant. The Jap attack split and went around the third battalion defenders who hung on with grim determination.

As daylight began to filter in, we could assess the mess below. Marine infantry reserves moved up to finish off the Japanese attack and come to the relief of the surrounded artillerymen. Some of our people from the second Battalion scrambled down the hillside to the flat and helped with the cleanup. The devastation was terrible. When the Japanese hit the poorly situated 27th, they rolled up several units that took off for the rear, including the captain who jumped in our CP. But a lot of the 27th stuck to their guns and fought to the death. Here and there were dead defenders grouped around a machine gun or an automatic rifle, men who got outflanked, surrounded, fought and died. It was almost enough to bring tears into our eyes.

We had a lot of buddies in the Third Battalion and we sought information on their whereabouts. One career regular, Lt. Hofstedder had recently transferred from the Second to the Third Battalion and inquiries were made about his whereabouts. A squint-eyed, mud-spattered staff sergeant said: "Oh, yeah. Hofstedder led the defense. He is out there with a loader and a machine gun." He pointed to a ditch bisecting the body-strewn field in front.

Our guys moved across the field to find Hofstedder and his machine gun set up in the mouth of the ditch, originally a Japanese tank trap. Under cover of darkness, the Jap attackers had been trotting unseen up the ditch, which came close to the Army line, then breaking out on a screaming run at elements of the

27th. When the 27th was overrun, Hofstedder realized that survival of the Third Battalion depended on stopping the Japs at the point where they were coming up the ditch. He picked up a .30 caliber machine gun and a crew with all the ammo boxes they could carry and led a dash across the field straight at the Japs. They reached the mouth of the ditch, set up the machine gun and began delivering a withering fire into the swarming enemy.

As our guys got to the tank trap, they found the Lieutenant calmly smoking a cigar, one hand resting on his now silent weapon. "Look at 'em," Hofstedder waved a hand at the tangle of dead enemy piled up in the ditch. "They're all mine."

The attack on the 27th was the last gasp on Saipan for the defending Japanese. That final Banzai charge used up most of their remaining troops. Resistance was relatively meager from then until our troops swept to the end of the a island and Division command announced the target "secured."

Of course, the fact that the island was secured did not automatically end all the violence. There were several hundred Japanese defenders hiding out in the thickets, ravines and caves and all resistance would not end until weeks later. But the main battle for Saipan was finished. From the scarred, shell-torn terrain on the side of Mt. Tapotcho, we looked out across the blue ocean and watched fliers, sailors and shore personnel swimming off the reefs and diving off the wings of PBY planes moored in the bay below.

Cruisers and battleships loomed on the horizon, just hanging off there like mobile forts. Somewhere out of sight we knew were a fleet of aircraft carriers. Small boats cruised up and down. Destroyers cut wakes, checking the waters below for any Jap submarines brave enough or foolish enough to try their luck with our fleet. Truck traffic was endless, supplies slithering uphill through the muck from where merchant ships were unloading in Garapan Harbor. The place was busy.

Several hundred mud-spattered, scraggly-bearded Marines

went about their jobs, cleaning and oiling the artillery pieces, cleaning and oiling rifles, washing up in helmets full of rainwater. A few guys built small fires, heated water and actually shaved. There was not a whole lot of talk going on. The elation over wrapping up this strategic Japanese base and burying its elite defenders was tempered by the carnage we had witnessed and the memory of the comrades we lost.

Somebody said the Battalion Chaplain was holding services in a big tent in an adjacent Jap farmyard, so most of us got up, sauntered over to bow our heads and thank God that we were still alive. More than 200 rifle-toting Marines filtered into the tent for the service as we arrived. One of the first men I recognized was an old buddy from Fox Battery, Corporal Cecil Shufelt, who yelled all the way across the tent: "Cary! How the hell did you make it this far?"

This reference to Hades elicited a considerable amount of subdued laughter; but the seriousness of what we had just gone through was ever present. When the Chaplain brought the service together with the Lord's Prayer, there was no levity in the tent. We all knew how close we had been to being buried with our fallen comrades in the hills and swamps beyond the tent. We listened silently and intently as the Chaplain delivered a terse, pertinent message. I cannot recall the sermon in its entirety, or even the major part of it. I do recall that he ended by pointing out that one cannot make a greater personal sacrifice than to lay down his life for another and that we were gathered to pray for our fallen comrades: "Those Marines," the Chaplain said, "Who lay down their lives that the rest of us might live."

With the benediction, we filed silently out of the tent. Another 200 Marines were gathered outside for a second service and many of them called to us as we left. Few answered. We were immersed in our own thoughts. We carried a heavy burden of grief.

Chapter 22
One More Invasion

The day Saipan was officially secured we were gathered around a radio Jeep listening to the Tokyo Rose radio show. The renegade Portland-born Rose had somehow wound up in Japan when the war broke out and was induced to cast her lot with the Emperor. She became a famous and entertaining propagandist for the Japanese Greater East Asia Co-Prosperity Sphere, which was what the Japanese military called their attempt to occupy most of the real estate bordering the Pacific Ocean. Rose had an extensive library of American jazz records and broadcast a lot of music out of the Big Band Era which she interspersed with dire predictions concerning the fate of any troops foolish enough to oppose Japanese military might.

First Sergeant Bittick, shirt off and smoking a cigar, was sitting in the front seat of the radio Jeep, fiddling with the volume button when Rose came on. Bittick leaned back to enjoy the music while the rest of us crowded around. A couple of songs were played and then Rose spoke in her soft, feminine voice: "You Marines of the Second and Fourth Divisions may think you won a great victory on Saipan, but the fight is not over. A huge naval task force with thousands of Japanese troops is steaming toward the island at this very moment and will sweep you into the sea. Sorry to say, but none of you Marines will ever get home for another Christmas."

Bittick took a pull on his cigar, blew out a cloud of blue smoke and addressed the radio: "Send 'em down, Rose. We just laid out 25,000 of your best troops and we'll be glad to lay out another 25,000 if they land here."

It was true. We had wiped out over 25,000 tough Japanese defenders. Nearly 7,000 Marines had gone down in the process. But those of us who were left felt just a little cocky. We had met their best and defeated them totally; however, the job wasn't quite finished. The word came down that we had two weeks to get geared up for the invasion of Tinian, a slightly smaller island that lay in plain view across two miles of blue Pacific water.

Along with our casualties, there were a number of victims of dengue fever, numerous recurring malaria cases and a lot of dysentery, the eternal affliction of troops since war was invented. Still, we had time to wash our clothes, shave, shower, eat a few meals of real food, re-build our ammunition supply and replace missing or broken equipment. We could not understand, however, what the urgency was about capturing Tinian. From reading maps, we knew Tinian had a large airfield. We knew it once held a fairly large fleet of fighter planes that had been wiped out by our Navy in earlier raids.

"What's the rush about going into Tinian?" several tired Marines asked.

"Because it's there and the Japs own it," was the standard answer. Right!

Jarheads on the ground were not privy to the grand strategy. The allied command determined Tinian had the terrain required for construction of an airfield that would accommodate the huge new B-29 bombers coming from the states. We could not comprehend why there was no time to totally fill our depleted ranks with reinforcements, but once we were re-supplied, we geared up, buckled our helmet straps, shouldered our packs and headed for the LST's which would be waiting to haul us to the assault point.

In most invasions, we anticipated screw-ups of varying degree due to poor intelligence, bad planning, or both, but this was one invasion where the Marine Corps pulled off a piece of brilliance. Aerial reconnaissance showed there was only one beach on Tinian Island suitable for a mass landing. It was a beach with a wide sand strip lying directly in front of the capitol city, Tinian Town. The city backed up against a sheer rock cliff which aerial recon revealed as honeycombed with tunnels, each one containing artillery, 90mm anti-aircraft guns or machine guns. Their ground forces consisted of somewhere between 6,000 and 10,000 infantry, artillerymen and tankers. Storming up that heavily defended beach would be a very costly enterprise. With our decimated ranks, there was doubt we could even pull it off. The balance of the island's shoreline, however, was sheer rock, rising straight up from the ocean to heights of a hundred feet or more... except for one small place.

Aerial recon seemed to indicate a small crack in the rock wall on the northwest, a crack that was not visible from the water. To check this out, a team of scouts went ashore in darkness by rubber boat, spent several nights prowling around the north end of the island, eventually coming back out, undetected by the enemy. They inspected the crack in the rock bluff, a short, meandering path just wide enough to accommodate one tank, one truck, or a squad of infantrymen at a time. It was lightly defended with only a few shore guns and some small arms. The Japanese did not believe we would attack at that point and had everything they owned down at Tinian Town. It was decided to filter part of the two Marine divisions though that crack on July 24, and just to make sure the Japs didn't jam the works, an elaborate fake was arranged off the beach of Tinian Town.

On July 24, much of the fleet lay offshore from Tinian Town, hammering the rock walls and caves above. Dive-bombers screamed in, unloading tons of 500-pound bombs. Transports discharged a large fleet of amtracs filled with Marines. The tractors churned around, forming into attack lines, then circled and reformed again. The defending Japs were pretty cagey and didn't waste much time on the theatrical event, instead saving their ammo for our troops when they hit the beach. About the only real excitement was when several of our warships steamed in for some point blank firing which drew a response from the shore guns above the town. Several hits were registered on the Battleship Colorado, which was nearly disabled and had to be towed back out to sea. But the ruse worked.

At the same time all this was going on, elements of the Second and Fourth Divisions began filtering in through the crack to the northwest. Our Marine amphib tractor force had been so decimated in the Saipan invasion that we were taken in by the Army. In addition, our officer corps had been severely depleted on Saipan. The invasion had a new commander, Major General Harry Schmidt, over both the Second and Fourth Divisions. What was left of two divisions was merged into one single attack unit. It fell to elements of the former Fourth Division to make the initial assault. Artillery support would be from us, the Second Battalion Tenth, which now had a new commander, Major David Henderson, who replaced the wounded Col. Shell. What few new people we received were given crash courses on assault procedure, how our 75mm howitzers were sighted, loaded, locked and fired. And we tried to infuse the replacements with some sense of what was about to happen and how they would be expected to perform under fire.

"Jig Day" on Tinian (to differentiate from Dog-Day on

194

Saipan) dawned clear on July 24. Our Army-driven amtracs rolled out of the bows of the LST's and started forming up for the run to shore. Our driver was all excited. "Wait until I write home to my folks that I took my tractor into Tinian loaded with Mo-rines!" he exulted. It was his first combat landing. We hoped it wouldn't be his last.

Intermittent fire from a five-inch Jap defense gun whined around us as we churned toward the landing point. Most of this stuff splashed into the sea, sending up white geysers of foam, nothing like the roaring hell on the beaches of Saipan. There were perhaps five amphibs ahead of ours, all carrying Fourth Division riflemen. About 200 yards off shore, there was a heck of an explosion ahead of us as one amphib took a direct hit. There was a huge puff of grayish-white smoke, then nothing. The smoke blew a way and there was simply nothing there. No wreckage, no personnel in the water. Nothing. A rocket ship curved in off our port side and fired several banks of missiles that raked the bluff above the landing zone. We received no more fire from that particular gun but it had done its damage.

Our tractor ground onto the beach, wound up the rock-walled corridor and stopped on a mesa above. As we vaulted over the side, we caught glimpses of the vast flat grasslands marking the airfield, bombed-out remains of Jap planes in concrete revetments along the runways and green groves of trees a mile ahead. Elements of the Fourth Division fanned out on our right, sweeping ahead between the sea and us. We jogged inland to a slight rise and ducked down to catch our breath. So far, the invasion was going off like clockwork. There had been only occasional small arms fire and the attack was rolling. We knew the balance of our division would be coming in behind us to sweep across the airfield and take up positions on our left. We were aware from radio communication that the Japanese defenders had begun streaming north from Tinian Town, furious at being misled about the landing and would attempt to knock us off the island after dark. Dive-bombers and fighters from our aircraft carriers were passing overhead, ranging south to pour harassing fire on the advancing enemy.

A few hundred yards ahead, our scouts picked out a solid defensive position where a road and a rail line intersected. Orders came down for us to move up and secure the crossroads for our first night's defense line. It was a steaming hot afternoon, the men were tired and a lot of them were not fully recovered from three weeks of war on Saipan. First Sergeant Bittick came loping along the rise, waving his carbine and urging everyone to get up and get going. "Move out!" Bittick yelled. "Move out! You can't live forever!"

Most of the men struggled up and began jogging ahead. A few still lagged in the dirt. "O.K., you heard it!" I yelled. "Everybody move out!" With that, I began kicking at the boot soles of those lying on the ground. One by one, they got up, except for one guy who didn't move even when I kicked his boots. The next kick I put in his the middle of his backpack and as he rolled slightly forward, his helmet came off revealing a bullet hole through his forehead. I looked around with a sick feeling, but nobody else saw it. The dead guy was not from our company. He was probably a Fourth Division scout that got tagged by a sniper earlier. I felt awful about kicking him, but nothing could be done. I shrugged it off, ran and caught up with my squad.

The two embankments where the road and the railroad intersected offered excellent cover. On top of that, there was a big field of what looked like turnips in front - about 200 acres - that presented a flat, unobstructed field of fire. We got our flanking outpost machine guns in place, dug individual foxholes along the embankment and got ready for the attack. Air recon reported the Jap forces now streaming up the roads toward us figured to arrive sometime before midnight. The information proved accurate.

Gunnery Sergeant Hogue came by, looking over our defenses, making a few suggestions and checking to see that everyone had plenty of ammo and grenades. Outside of a few chickens picking around, it was pretty quiet out on the farmland and if it hadn't been that a war was going on, it would have been a pleasant afternoon. Hogue and I stood on the embankment looking things over when he suddenly pointed to our right and growled: "For cripes sake, look at that!"

Headquarters personnel from one battalion of the Fourth Division had moved in to set up defenses, but somebody in the group apparently didn't think there was a real war going on. A group of Marines had been ordered to erect a huge canvas command tent right out in the open. Part of the crew were busy filling sandbags, which were being stacked up as a wall around the tent.

"Migod!" Hogue barked. "Those guys are looking to draw artillery fire." He shook his head and started back toward our battalion HQ that was dug into the railroad embankment. Before Hogue went 20 steps, three Jap shells screamed in from what sounded like 90mm dual-purpose guns and smacked the tent dead center. A few more screeched in and then the firing stopped. When the smoke and dust cleared, the tent was nothing but a bundle of smoking rags. They had plenty of help with the casualties so we didn't go over there, but we heard that a dozen guys got hit and the battalion lost just about its whole command structure. Tribute to a dumb choice of a tent site.

About midnight, we began to hear the enemy assembling in the darkness beyond the turnip field. There was a lot of yelling and blowing of whistles as the officers got the troops in line for the attack. It sounded like Pickett getting ready to charge at Gettysburg. Indeed, it took them so long to get ready some of our people fell asleep. But we were all jerked wide awake when the first shouts of "Banzai! Banzai!" echoed across the turnip field. At that point, the Navy fired a string of star shells along the line, lighting up the scene like daylight.

For anyone who had never seen one, a Banzai charge was an awesome sight with hundreds of men racing forward, bayonets gleaming in the night, officers in front waving two-handed swords and the whole bunch screaming their heads off. At 200 yards, we cut loose. Our two machine guns were set for a cross fire at knee height and the attack ran right between them. The first blast knocked down a whole row of running troops including the commander, a major who took a burst across his ankles. In a moment, he was back up, waving his sword, screaming and limping on the bloody stubs of his legs. The second burst caught him chest-high and his war was over.

Between the star shells, the yammering machine guns, strings of tracers and rifle fire, the scene was total chaos. Only one live enemy made it to where I was dug in. He was sprinting at a crouch, zigzagging, and I had trouble trying to get a bead on him. Suddenly, he hit the road embankment next to me and leaped over. It was then that I saw he was not even carrying a weapon, just running and yelling. Before I could snap a shot off, he vanished behind me. I grabbed a field phone and hollered to the battery in back of us. "Hey, one just got through…he's coming your way!" There was a flurry of rifle fire and a voice on the phone said: "We nailed him…and guess what? He didn't have a rifle!" In the chaos of war, it was something for which there was no answer.

After the first volley of fire by our automatic weapons, the attack faltered and broke down. The enemy hit the ground and began crawling toward us, which didn't work, either because they were exposed out in the turnip field. Some flattened out behind dead comrades and started returning our fire. Two Jap light machine guns opened up and began spraying our part of the embankment, kicking up dirt and sending strings of tracers arching into the night. I eased my head up over the rim of the embankment to get a fix on this problem and the string of tracers swung right at me. Whether he spotted my helmet or was just sweeping our position, I couldn't tell, but I pulled my head in like a startled turtle.

In the middle of this melee, Corporal Mike Vaughan, who was manning the outpost machine gun on our left, called in yelling he was out of ammo and to cover him and his loader who were coming in. Everybody with a rifle opened up, pinning the enemy as the two gunners sprinted to the railroad embankment and dropped behind it. But Vaughan wasn't done. He and his loader dodged around, found all the boxes of machine gun ammo they could carry, asked for more covering fire and sprinted back out to their gun. In all the excitement, the Japs didn't know they were gone. Vaughan got the Browning chattering again and pretty well finished off the attack single-handed. We heard later that he was cited for a Silver Star.

Eventually, the battle simmered down to a few scattered rifle pops and then silence, except for stray incoming Japanese artillery. As daylight filtered in over the turnip patch, we came out of our holes, formed a thin skirmish line and worked our way across the field. There had been about 3,000 Japanese in the banzai attack and 1500 were dead in our sector, 300 stacked up directly in front of the embankment. Following standard procedure, we moved out to check the dead enemy, to kick them and make sure they were all dead and stayed dead. Live Japanese soldiers would sometimes feign death, lying face down, hands holding grenades beneath them. When a Marine walked past they would hurl a grenade at his back. Thus it became a regular ritual to check out all the dead and take no chances.

We found no live enemy in the midst of all that bloody carnage. We leaned on our rifles and gazed around in sort of a half-stunned stupor as the sun came up. Paul Ryan, who had taken a mortar hit on Saipan and had no love for Japanese troops anyway, stared slowly right and left at the sprawled dead, pulled out a cigarette and lit it up. "These guys look like they are all from the same family," Ryan growled, aiming his cigarette at the sprawled figures. "I bet they are all named Watanabe." This generated a few laughs that somewhat alleviated the fatigue and adrenalin-pumped tenseness from the firefight. There was a certain relief in just being alive and able to look a all the destruction around us. We could not help but think that a few hours before; these were live men, fired up to attack and kill us. Now they were reduced to motionless bundles of bloody, khaki rags.

Gunnery Sergeant Hogue came over and said we were getting ready to move out but we had to find some fresh ammunition first. "You see any of those Army amphibs loaded with ammo?" Hogue asked.

"Not since we came in yesterday." I looked back toward the landing site. "The last ones I saw were back on the ridge above the beach."

Hogue signaled to follow and we headed back toward the landing site. Sure enough, sitting in the sand just inland from the crack in the rock, were a dozen Army amphibs but with no one around. Hogue scrambled up to make sure they contained ammunition, then dropped back down and swore up a storm. "They're full of ammo but where the hell are all the drivers?"

With that, there was a shuffling under the nearest amphib. A very young Army Staff Sergeant crawled out, brushing sand from his pants.

"What's up, doc" the Staff quipped, grinning.

Hogue wasn't smiling. "We are getting ready to move out," he said, pointing toward our position. "You better get this ammo up to our people."

The Staff Sergeant, still grinning, shook his head. "No, man. We ain't goin' up there. They're shootin' up there."

"Nobody's shooting now," Hogue argued.

"That don't mean they can't start," the Staff Sergeant countered.

"Listen!" Hogue bellowed in frustration. "You better get that that stuff up to us or the Japs will be right down here with you! Make up your mind!"

The Staff Sergeant thought it over for a second, than kneeled down and yelled under the amphib. "Get out of there you dogfaces! We gotta get this stuff up to them Marines!"

Not only from under that amphib, but also from under the others, bunches of soldiers came crawling out. When the firefight started during the night, they apparently crawled underneath the amphibs and flattened out between the armored tracks. If they thought those were places of safety, they weren't. One Jap grenade in any one of those ammo-loaded amphibs would have sent it to the moon and probably fried the troops underneath.

In a couple of minutes, all the tractors were belching exhaust and lurching forward. Hogue and I led them to the crossroads where everybody stocked up on cartridges and got ready to move out. Trucks and jeeps hooked onto the artillery pieces and began hauling them southbound, down the road. Some of us rode on the trucks, some walked. It was a slow procession as we moved through farms and orchards. Our officers had a problem keeping the troops from breaking ranks and running over to the fruit groves to grab papaya melons or stalks of bananas. Within an hour, all the troops in the column had packsacks bulging with melons or were carrying stalks of bananas over their shoulders as they moved along.

We stopped at one large farmyard for a breather, sat down and drank from our canteens. And we talked about the night before. One of our radio men related an interesting tale about how, when the Jap attack was finally stopped, several battalions were ordered to counterattack. He was listening to the radio transmissions and the colonel in charge of the counterattack got angry because one company didn't move out. He yelled the company call sign, got an answer and said: "Dog Company, get the attack going."

The reply came back: "Sir, we can't attack. We have only a dozen men left to cover a hundred yard front. We are lucky just to hold on."

"Who am I talking to?" the colonel bellowed.

"Corporal Jennings, sir."

"Listen, corporal, you put on your company commander!"

"Sir," came the quiet reply. "I am the company commander."

There was a moment of awkward silence, then the colonel came back on the radio, his voice somewhat softer. "Just hang on there, son. We'll send some people over to give you a hand."

Not everybody came through the firefight unscathed.

Chapter 23
Tinian Mop Up

From the middle of the island, through the last five miles, the fighting got bitter. The Japs were excellent on defense, digging in for concealment, making use of all the natural rock and vegetation features of the land. But by now we had Tinian Town and its docks which allowed supplies to come pouring in, especially artillery ammo. It was like the Division didn't want any shells left over to transport someplace else. We fired nonstop into anything that looked like an enemy position. If an infantry squad got hung up even briefly, our forward observers called in: "Battalion! Five rounds! Fire for effect!"

Five rounds of high explosive. With twelve 75's in the battalion, that was 60 shells crashing into the enemy position. We were not just pushing the enemy back, we were obliterating him. The joke was going around that we were spending about $200,000 a Jap to get rid of them and if we gave each one $10,000 in cash and a ticket back to Tokyo it would probably be cheaper and a lot less dangerous for everybody.

On top of firepower, we had total air and sea control. We could call in air strikes or navy shellfire whenever a serious problem arose. In spite of the rough, rocky, tunnel-holed terrain, the enemy was getting pounded. Periodically, we were hit with banzai attacks, which invariably ended with a lot of dead enemy. And then it started raining. It rained for several days and nights straight which made it very difficult to operate. We slopped around in the mud wearing our rubberized ponchos, attempting to keep our guns and gear fairly dry and still trying to fight a war. Every night we tensed up, expecting another banzai attack. From footprints in the muck we knew a lot of Japs were moving around at night, filtering past our outposts.

One night, as sergeant of the guard, I drew the midnight-to-four a.m. watch. We were in rolling farmland, a mixture of vegetable fields, fruit trees and thick stands of sugar cane fringed by rocky ridges and dense scrub forests. Just to the south of our company position was a huge stand of cane which could provide cover for half the Jap army if it took a notion to attack. We had a .30 caliber machine gun set up on a small rise overlooking the sugar cane and we fired it in before dark, setting the elevation on the traverse bar. If an attack came in the dark, all the gunner had to do was hold down the trigger and swing the muzzle back and forth. The gun would do the rest. The outpost gunner on my watch was a young kid named Henry Bauslaugh. He was hunkered over the machine gun, trying to shelter it with his poncho as the eternal rain pelted down. It must have been maybe two in the morning when the telephone line from Bauslaugh crackled in the command post. "Sarge," he whispered hoarsely. "We got a bunch of 'em coming."

I hustled out of the pit and made my way carefully to the ridge where the kid was manning the machine gun. As I slid in alongside him, he said: "Listen! There must be a whole battalion coming."

It was true. In the interminable darkness stretching out before us, we could hear a host of bodies slopping and clumping through the wet sugar cane. On the field phone, I whispered back to the command post and got the duty officer. "Looks like we have a major attack," I murmured. "We'll need a lot of help up here in a hurry. Over and out."

I knew the duty officer would roust out the company. I only hoped Bauslaugh and I could stop or slow down the attack long enough for them to get up to us. The thought flashed through my mind that maybe this was it. Maybe my time was up. But I had thought that a hundred times before, so I dismissed it. It was time to fight. Bauslaugh tightened up as the first footsteps came out of the sugar cane and started up the hill toward us. I was holding the poncho over the gun with one hand, set to feed the ammo belt with my other. I flipped the poncho off to free both hands and said tersely: "Let 'er go, Henry!"

In the pitch-black downpour, blinding yellow flame shot out of the machine gun muzzle. There was massive crashing of bodies going down in the inky darkness as Bauslaugh steadily traversed the gun back and forth. And then, over the hammering gun, a weird sound reached my ears. I gripped Henry's arm and yelled in his ear: "Cut it out! Stop firing!"

He hammered off a few more rounds and then reluctantly released the trigger. From the darkness below we heard not only the flailing of wounded bodies in the mud but a whole chorus of Moo! Moo! Moo! In the dark, we had ripped into a whole herd of approaching cows.

The duty officer slogged up with a bunch of riflemen about the time a mortar crew sent several flares up over the scene. The duty officer, Colt.45 in his hand, stared at the mess and said the obvious: "Migod, you guys shot up a whole herd of cows."

"Yeah, but they're Japanese cows," Henry said. For one thing we were sure: the cooks would make good use of the beef.

One of our biggest concerns on Tinian involved the thousands of Japanese civilians. They were terrified, not just from the war itself, but from propaganda fed them by the Japanese high command, propaganda to the effect that we would torture and kill all civilians, even kids. A lot of the people were so frightened they hurled their children off the cliffs, much of it at a place called Marpo Point at the south end of the island. The parents jumped after the kids, piling up on the rocks below. It was horrifying. We had Japanese-American civil affairs people on loudspeakers, pleading with the civilians to come in. We had civil affair people on boats just offshore shouting at the Japanese that they would be given food, water and shelter and would be treated humanely. Still, they kept jumping. The soldiers were different. Some of the enemy troops blew themselves up with hand grenades, an activity, which met with our universal approval. Several hundred others vanished into the sugar cane fields and jungle ravines where they played deadly hide-and-seek with our forces for more than a month.

As the end of organized resistance approached on Tinian, it got tougher and tougher to ferret the enemy out of the caves and tunnels in the cliffs. Also, we sensed victory was at hand and those of us lucky enough to be alive grew cagier about sticking our necks out more than necessary. We slowed down and used our heads and our equipment rather than the old "gung ho" attitude.

On patrol one afternoon, Swanson and I led our men around the bend of a small roadway carved out of a cliff and found one of our 75mm howitzer crews parked on a small ledge. We didn't know any of our crews were that far forward and we inquired as to what the heck they were doing out there alone. "Looking for targets," one gunner laughed.

"Who's calling fire? " Swanson asked.

"We call our own," said the gunner. "See that cave across the canyon?" he pointed to a big hole on the far side of the ravine.

"Yeah, we see it,"

"That's a cave with a bunch of Japs hiding out in there. Every now and then one or two of them come sneaking out and we nail 'em."

"With the 75?"

"Yeah, with the 75."

Swanson and I stood there in disbelief. We lit up a couple of cigarettes, sat down on rocks and watched. "Hey, here comes one now," a guy with field glasses whispered.

First there was a shadow moving at the mouth of the cave, then an enemy soldier come easing out cautiously, a rifle in one hand, the other wiping sweat off his forehead with a handkerchief.

"Fire!" barked the crew chief. The gunner jerked the lanyard and the gun recoiled with a loud bang. The Jap at the mouth of the cave simply vanished in a cloud of smoke and flying dirt.

"Bingo!" muttered the gunner.

Swanson and I kept the patrol moving, leaving the gun crew to work on the cave. War, we agreed, is a weird, violent and uncomprehending business.

After nine days, the island was ruled "secured." Something like 6,000 Japanese soldiers had been destroyed and almost 10,000 civilians taken prisoner. Our command listed 1,100 Marine casualties. We immediately got busy with civilian work crews smoothing gravel on the airfield and on the roads leading from Tinian Town. For several days, my squad handled 30 civilians laborers, mostly elderly men and a few teen-age kids. One of the teens, a pleasant-faced young man named Hashimoto, had a good command of English which he said he learned in school. He was my go-between, relaying orders to the rest of the work crew. Early on, we had been warned to look out for Jap soldiers who may have thrown away their uniforms and melted into the civilian population.

One day, we were spreading gravel near the edge of a farmyard and one of the workers, who appeared to be about 25 years of age, was goofing off. Not really working. I told Hashimoto to tell the malingerer to get busy. Hashi seemed wary of the guy and I began to keep an eye on him. He was at an odd age for a civilian. Paul Ryan came over with a five-gallon can of drinking water for the crew and I told Paul of my suspicions about the cork-off. "I'll take care of it," Paul said tersely. He walked over to the Jap, who was leaning on his shovel; grinning and watching the others work.

"Hey!" Paul said. "Get moving! Get the gravel shoveled!"

The Jap looked at Paul and shrugged like he didn't understand. "I said for you to get busy," Paul growled, pointing the muzzle of his Garand at the guy's forehead. "Or I am gonna blow your damn head off!" The Jap began shoveling gravel at a furious pace.

"That bugger can understand English," Paul said. "And I think he's a soldier."

After work, as we unloaded our two truckloads of laborers at the internment camp, I told a civil affairs officer that I thought we had a soldier mixed in with our workers. "That one," I said, pointing at the surly Jap climbing down from the truck. The civil affairs officer and an M.P went over, collared the guy and took him in for interrogation. The officer came back in a few minutes. "You were right, he is a soldier."

I felt better about getting him locked up. Those guys were bitter enders and you never knew what they might try. However, ex-soldiers weren't the only problem. We had one army civil affair captain who walked over to talk with a 14 year-old youngster and they both went sky high when the kid set off a charge of dynamite tied around his body under his jacket.

One day, when were working on the road, a grizzled, gray-haired old Jap with a scraggly mustache shambled over to me, something cupped in his hands. I was sitting on the ground half awake, my back against a coconut tree and my rifle in my lap.

The old man kept coming, bowing and mumbling something in Japanese. I didn't pay too much attention until he was almost on top of me and then I spotted the hand grenade he was holding. I swung my rifle around quickly and told him to back away. His eyes grew huge and he began to shake. Hashimoto came running over and I told him to tell the old man to back off and lay the grenade down, which he did. I went over for a look. It was an American grenade which had been armed and thrown but had failed to explode. These things were always touchy and you never knew what might set one off. I told Hashi to tell the rest of the crew that if they found any more unexploded ordnance, to let it alone and tell me where it was so I could mark it. In no instance were they to pick any of that stuff up and bring it to me. Frankly, that old man just about scared the poop out of me. I suppose I scared the poop out of him, too.

One day, when we were working on the airfield, we heard an incredible roar of engines. Over the treetops swept several gleaming, new B-29 bombers, huge planes, the ones that would be used to carry the mail to the Japanese homeland. My civilian crew stopped working to watch in amazement and then Hashi came running over to ask what those planes were. "New B-29's," I said.

"What are you going to do with them?" he asked.

"They're going to bomb Tokyo."

Hashi's eyes grew huge and he ran back to the work crew. There was a lot of jabbering and I heard the word "Tokyo" mentioned several times. Hashi came running back and bowed politely. "Really going to Tokyo?" he asked.

"Yeah, really," I said.

Hashi thought this over and then asked an odd question: "What are you Marines doing here?"

"We are fixing up the airfield." I was puzzled. "Why?"

"But what are you doing on Tinian?"

This was even more puzzling. "We need the island because

of the big airfield."

"Yes, but why would you be fighting out here when we have already captured Hawaii and are fighting on the west coast of America?"

I studied Hashi for a minute. "Is that what your government has been telling you?"

"Is not so?" Hashi came back.

"No, not so. This war is almost over, Hashi, and Japan has lost. The Germans are surrendering. The war is winding down. Another island or two and our troops will be in Japan itself."

Hashi stared at me. I could see the wheels going around inside his head. For years the Japanese propaganda machine had been telling the Japanese people that they were winning the war. All of a sudden, a bunch of Marines show up in Hashimoto's home island and he had trouble figuring out what we were doing there. He looked at me for a moment then walked back to the work crew. I could see he was agitated, waving his arms as he tried to explain all this to them. The civilians looked first at Hashi, then at me, then back at Hashi, then at the B-29's. I don't know how much they believed, but the appearance of the B-29's without any opposition must have had an impact.

The Army came in when the island was secured and took over all operations. Orders were given for all Marine units to be shipped to Saipan where we would re-outfit and train for the next invasion. The only clinker was, the whole division got transferred to Saipan except the Second Battalion 10th. Somewhere the orders got screwed up and we were left on Tinian. It wasn't bad there. We had a bivouac set high up on a mesa atop a huge cliff overlooking a sea of sugar cane fields. At night it was cool there. The main problem was that the Army controlled all the supplies. Our rations normally came through the Navy over at Saipan. Our new battalion commander, Col. Henderson, had a sizzling word war going with Division command on Saipan. Henderson was asking how the heck we were supposed to eat.

Division said they were going to ship us back to join with the main force at Saipan right away. But right away didn't happen.

On top of that, there were still a pretty fair number of enemy troops hiding out on the island and we were making daily patrols, digging them out of the caves and sugar cane fields. On one patrol, we cornered a half dozen in a cane field. We knew the number from their footprints. There had been a fresh rain and their tell-tale tracks from split-toed sneakers were quite evident. We set up two teams to bag them. Half of the Marines formed a skirmish line and moved into the cane field slowly. The rest of us got on a slight ridge overlooking the field. The plan was for the skirmishers to flush them into us where we could capture or shoot them.

These Japs were not the surrendering kind. When they realized they were being pinched off between two lines they put up a fight, hurling hand grenades at the skirmishers.

"Porky" LaVelle, a somewhat beefy guy, was point man when the Nips started hurling grenades. Porky spotted them and started firing. One of the grenades landed by Porky's feet and rolled past him. He simply hunched, took the blast, but kept on firing his rifle, knocking down all six of the enemy. The rest of us moved in to mop up but not much mopping up was needed. Porky did a good job, but paid for it.

"Geez, you been hit," somebody said, noticing a rapidly-growing splotch of blood spreading out on the back of Porky's pants..

"Yeah," he said, matter-of-fact. "The buggers nicked me."

It was more than a nick. We put first aid bandages on the wounds, helped him to a Jeep and drove him back to the battalion aid station. From there they sent him to a hospital ship in the bay. "Porky's got him a ticket home," somebody said.

In addition to the problems of trying to find food on an island that was filling up with supplies we couldn't get our hands on, we were getting replacements in from the states. One of these was a bright young lieutenant named Smits, a kid no more than 21. He was fresh from Officer's Candidate School, had a brand new Colt .45 and was dying to shoot it at somebody. About the third day he was in the company, I drew him on a patrol. Usually, we were assigned half a square mile to patrol, hiking the roads around the perimeter of the area and inspecting any abandoned Jap emplacements that look like they could be back in use. In actual practice, I took my patrols out behind the nearest hills and sat down out of sight to smoke cigarettes and shoot the breeze. As far as we were concerned, our war on Tinian was over and we weren't going to get any more people banged up hunting trouble. We figured the new Army troops coming in should share in that glory.

Anyway, I picked up my orders from Captain Finn and also the additional company of Lt. Smits. His eyes were dancing and he was all excited to be going on his first honest-to-God patrol against an enemy. And that was scary in itself. He wanted a firefight and we didn't. The thing was, our bivouac was up on a mesa and the area we were to patrol was in the farm flats below so we had to wind our way down a steep path to the cane fields. From below, we could not see the tents above. Just the edge of the cliff. I let Smits go first and then fell in at the rear of the patrol. We had gone only a few hundred yards when word came back: "Sarge, get up to the front of the column!"

I hustled past the squad, strung out along the road, and found Smits studying a map. "What's the matter sergeant? Are you afraid?" he blurted out.

I looked at him not quite understanding what he was really saying. Two of the patrol were standing nearby, watching and grinning. "Afraid of what, sir?" I asked.

"Why are you hanging out in the rear?"

"All patrols are led by the senior person, sir. The second in command always brings up the rear."

Smits glared at me: "Well I want you right up here with

me," he said.

It was then I realized he didn't have a clue where we were and couldn't figure out the map. The nearby guys were still grinning as I took over and led the patrol up one lane and down the next in a big circle, past a lot of sugar cane I was sure contained no hidden Japs. After a few hours, I led the men, plus Lt. Smits, back to the field below our battalion area. As we passed by the base of the cliff where our tents were situated, out of sight, Smits pointed to a series of old tunnels carved in the cliff, Japanese defenses, long abandoned. "What are those?" he asked.

"Jap tunnels, sir" I said.

"Don't you think we had better go in and check them out?" Smits asked.

It was clear the lieutenant had no idea that we were a few hundred feet directly below our battalion tent area. The rest of the squad had caught up and were watching all this drama with considerable interest.

"Sir," I said. "We don't just go strolling into those caves. Any Japs in there would have you silhouetted against the outside light and simply blow your guts out."

"What do we do then?" Smits asked.

"The usual procedure is to go after them with grenades," I said. "We toss in a phosphorus grenade - a smoke grenade - which burns like the devil. If there are any Japs in there they will start yelling. Then we toss in some high explosive grenades and clean them out."

"Do you have any grenades?" Smits asked.

"Just by chance I think we do," I said, signaling for Corporal Lowe to come over. "Jim, you got some smoke grenades?" I yelled in his good ear. His eardrum was blown out on the other side.

"Yeah," he grinned. "I got a couple."

"O.K. You come at that main cave from the right with smoke and I'll come in from the left with the H.E. The rest of the squad will deploy behind this line of rocks and give us cover. Toss in the smoke grenade and I'll follow with the high explosives stuff."

Smits was checking his .45 to make sure it was loaded. The squad was getting into this piece of theater in a big way. "Look," I said to the crew. "Corporal Lowe and I will sprint to the base of the cliff and hurl the grenades into the cave. If a bunch of Nips comes boiling out, make sure you get 'em all or Lowe and I will be dead meat!"

"We'll cover you, Sarge," a corporal said, trying to look grim, fingering his rifle. Smits knelt down tensely behind a boulder and pulled the hammer back on his .45. It was time for the curtain to go up on our show.

I looked down the line at the men, deployed and ready. Checked on Jim Lowe, then raised my hand like John Wayne attacking some renegade Indians. "Let's go!" I hissed at Jim. He nodded and took off for the cliff, circling in from the right while I zigzagged in from the left.

We dashed up to the base of the cliff, flattened dramatically against the rock face, and then edged our way along to the tunnel entrance. I raised my hand, just like in the movies, got a wave of assurance from Smits, and then signaled Lowe to throw his phosphorus grenade. He hurled it well back inside the cave where it went "poof" and sent a cloud of white smoke rolling out. It was time for the climax. I wound up to hurl the HE grenade into the tunnel but got distracted watching Smits below waving his pistol. My elbow hit a rock, the grenade bounced off the ledge above my head and began rolling back down the hill. "Grenade!" I yelled, flattening out against the ground.

Hand grenades don't usually make a huge noise, but this one seemed to go off like an atomic bomb. Maybe it was because things had been so quiet up to that point. The boom echoed off the cliffs and rang though the tent area above. Lowe and I ducked back down to the patrol and we all quickly melted away into the sugar cane as Col. Henderson, the exec officer and half

214

the battalion staff came charging downhill to find Lt. Smits standing alone with his .45 pistol. Witnesses said that Col. Henderson swore at Smits for five minutes without once repeating himself. The word got around about the grenade episode and at evening chow everybody was laughing up a storm.

Two days later, I drew another patrol. As I stood in Captain Finn's tent getting my orders, Lt. Smits walked in. He looked at me and I looked at him. His eyes narrowed when he became aware who was going on patrol with him. "We won't throw any grenades today, will we sergeant?" he said.

"No sir," I replied. And we didn't. Smits was learning. He would be O.K.

One morning Captain Finn sent for me. I had been on patrol the evening before. We had no officer on this trip so we did the usual thing. We went behind a big hill, sat down and smoked cigarettes. The problem was, somebody saw us and snitched to the captain who was pretty sore. "Sergeant," he said. "Where did you take that patrol yesterday?"

I rattled off the numbers of the roads we were supposed to have walked. Finn shook his head. "You never went there," he glowered. "You corked off. Swanson took his squad through that same area this morning and drew sniper fire."

I was tired, half sick with dengue fever and dysentery and didn't much care. "Captain," I said. "I got nine guys left in my squad, four of them from the old Guadalcanal team. Paul Ryan is still limping from the mortar that got him on Saipan. Dale Luttrell has a stiff left arm from an old sniper wound. Jim Lowe has one eardrum blown out. We are all sick and we are all tired. I am trying my best to get all those guys home in one piece. There must be somebody left in the United States who wants to come out and fight this damn war."

It was quite a speech. Finn glared at me but then his look softened. He ran a hand over his face "I know, sergeant, I know," he said and looked away. For a moment I thought I saw a tear in his eye. "Just do the best you can," he muttered, looked down and began shuffling some papers.

A couple days later, we were hiking a muddy road that looked safe, when one of our guys noted some fresh split-toed Jap tracks going into a sugar cane patch. We obviously had some enemy hidden out in the field next to us. What to do? It was a situation like the one where Porky LaVelle got hit. "Any volunteers to go in and flush those guys out?" I asked. Nobody seemed particularly eager to go.

"I got an idea," Jim Lowe said. "The Sea Bees are doing some road work with a couple of bulldozers a little way back. Let's get them to bulldoze the cane flat."

"Hey, they aren't gonna run those Japs out of there for us."

"We won't tell them there are Japs in the cane. We can tell 'em we need the area bulldozed flat because we are building a baseball field."

That sounded reasonable. Some of the guys hiked over to where the Sea Bees were working and explained we needed a baseball field. They were very cooperative and brought their machines over and started going back and forth, flattening the sugar cane. About the time we were getting down to the last few rows and figured the Japs would come out shooting, one of our guys spotted Jap tracks across the road from the field. There was a patch of gravel at the end of the field and the Jap's tracks weren't visible until we looked on the other side of the road.

"Sarge," one guy said. "The birds have flown. They were out of here before the Sea Bees even started on the sugar cane."

We thanked the Sea Bees and told them they could use our baseball field any time after we got it finished. I didn't really feel bad about not finding any Japanese. I reported back to Captain Finn that we saw some sign of enemy activity and marked the area on the map. I didn't tell him about the Sea Bees.

The next morning, about 10 a.m., I got a notice to report to the Captain's tent. As I walked up, Dale Luttrell was also arriving. "What the heck did we do wrong now?" Luttrell asked. I shrugged and we stepped inside. I thought maybe somebody told the Captain about the Sea Bees.

Captain Finn was sitting behind his small wooden desk, some papers in his hand. He gave one set to me and one to Luttrell. "What's this?" I asked.

"You're going home," Finn said, grinning.

Luttrell and I looked at each other and then at the papers. They were orders transferring us to the Naval hospital, Aieia Heights, Hawaii, for treatment of malaria and processing back to the states.

We were stunned. We just stood there trying to comprehend. Finn laughed. "It's real. You guys are flying out tomorrow morning. Be at the airfield with your papers and sea bags at 0800 hours."

We still couldn't believe it. When you have made up your mind over two and a half years that you are going to die in the south seas mud somewhere, it is stunning to find out you don't have too. Still, we were superstitious enough to figure something was sure to go wrong. Luttrell and I hurried back to our tents and started to pack our few possessions. The rest of the squad came over with congratulations and smacked us on our backs. We still kept thinking we were going to wake up and find we had one more patrol to make.

That evening was our last one in the Second Battalion chow line. As Headquarters and Service Company stood with our mess kits, waiting to get fried Spam and Japanese rice, a Jeep drove up and somebody let out a yell, "Hey! Porky LaVelle is back!"

It was true, LaVelle had gotten his grenade wounds patched up on the hospital ship and instead of going home, had been sent back to duty.

Burt Cox, a corporal from New York, who had a voice like a fog horn, bellowed:

"Hey, LaVelle! You've been recommended for the Congressional Medal of Honor!"

LaVelle was dumbfounded: "What for?" he asked.

"The Division Command figures all that iron you stopped with your big, fat butt could have killed a dozen officers," Cox yelled. The whole company roared with laughter. Even LaVelle laughed until tears ran down his face. It was a pretty happy supper. Particularly for Luttrell and me.

Chapter 24
The Tinian Food Patrol

Between the time hostilities ended on Tinian and Luttrell and I left for Hawaii, there was the fear of mass famine in the Second Battalion, Tenth Marines. Somehow, in the great scheme of military and naval planning, when the Second and Fourth Divisions were transferred back to Saipan, our battalion was overlooked in the program. Every other battalion in the two divisions was trucked to the new Army dock at Tinian Town, loaded onto LST's and taken the two miles across the bay to Saipan, which was being turned into a major Marine advanced base.

Except us. How the paperwork got so screwed up that we were left on Tinian, no one ever figured out, but it happened. The main issue involved food. All of our food supplies came through the Navy. The Army was in complete control of Tinian. We had no way of getting supplies through the Army, no matter how many radio messages were sent from our Battalion Command to Division Command on Saipan. Any direct attempt to beg Army supplies was met with a fish eye. Nobody in the Army was going to be responsible for doling out food to some Marine outfit and then having to explain it to higher authorities. Our cooks were down to some leftover cases of Spam and bags of Japanese rice, which we found stored in Japanese farm houses.

Captain Finn sent word down that he wanted me in his tent and I promptly obeyed. It may have been that Finn remembered our shoe heist in Hawaii and figured my squad probably had the most skillful thieves in the company.

"Sergeant," he said. "You know our food situation. We have scrounged up about all the papaya melons and bananas around here and we can't requisition any food from the Army. Do you have any ideas?"

"Yes sir. There is no question that the Army has plenty of food, probably a lot more than it will ever use. Give me two trucks and I'll take some men to see what we can do."

"All right, Sergeant, you've got the trucks. But remember: If you get caught, I don't know anything about it."

"I understand, sir."

Thus it was that Corporal Lowe and I got a pair of 3/4 ton trucks with drivers, a couple of more men from the squad and headed for the docks at Tinian Town. We were sure the fleet of cargo ships unloading there carried food supplies along with everything else. Our job would be to figure out how to sort out and acquire some food.

First, we determined to change our identity. We knew there was no way two Marine trucks were going to get onto the Army docks. We took some soft mud and smeared it over the Marine license numbers painted on the front bumpers of the two trucks. Then we took off our Marine dungaree jackets, operating with just our pants, so we looked like all the other grunts laboring in the heat. Guards rode the running boards on each side of the trucks, holding onto the windshields, rifles slung over their shoulders. We looked fairly official, exactly like the Army supply trucks. Then we drove downhill, picked up the road going to the dock and fell in line with several dozen Army trucks going the same way.

Alongside the ramp going to the dock was a staff sergeant with a clipboard and a pencil. He was marking down the identity of the Army trucks going past and waving them through. Until he hit us. With mud over our bumpers, there was no identity. "What outfit?" he yelled at us.

"Thirty-third Engineers!" I yelled back, figuring that sounded reasonable enough.

He studied his clipboard and couldn't find any 33rd Engineers. In the meantime, trucks were piling up behind us, beeping their horns. Frustrated, the staff sergeant waved us over to the side. "Listen, you guys wait and I'll check you later."

We drove to one side and then just kept going up the dock toward the cargo ships. The first two ships where we stopped were unloading clothing. We didn't need clothing. We kept moving, finally pulling up alongside a merchant ship that was tied up. A couple of sailors looked down from the deck above and asked what we wanted. "You guys got food supplies on board?" I yelled.

"Yeah, but we don't have orders to unload right now."

"Where's your Bosun's mate?" I asked.

"He's down below."

"Look, get him up on deck. We're Marines and we've got an emergency." Any time you wanted to get something done on a ship, you contacted the Bosun's mate. Whatever he said is what happened.

In two minutes, the "Boats" appeared, sleepily rubbing his eyes. "Whatta yuz want?" he muttered.

"Here's the picture" I yelled up. "We're from the Tenth Marines and we got stranded here when the Division went back to Saipan. We don't have any food and the Army won't give us any. Can you help us out?"

"Marines? You betcha buddy!" He turned back from the rail. "O.K., you swabbies! Hook a cargo net on the boom and start lifting food supplies up from the hold and over the side! Now, move it!"

In just minutes, a full cargo net of food cartons eased down to the dock. We grabbed the boxes and stowed them in the truck. The empty net went back up on the boom and a few minutes later it came down loaded again. We glanced at the cases, marked "Canned Beef," "Canned Corn," "Canned Beans," "Canned Peaches"... a whole gourmet assortment of real food. When we had the two trucks piled high with all they would hold, we waved our thanks to the sailors.

"Nice job you guys did on the island," the Bosun's Mate yelled down, referring to our battle on Tinian.

"We had a lot of help! " I yelled back.

Our drivers took our trucks across the dock, down another ramp to the road, then fell in line with a host of Army trucks and drove up the road away from Tinian Town. We came to a fork, one lane leading to our Battalion area, the other going to the Army supply dump. We peeled away from the caravan and drove to Captain Finn's tent.

The skipper came out with a broad grin on his face. "Good job." he laughed, looking over our load of loot.

"Had a little luck, sir."

About then, the Battalion Executive Officer showed up. He had a totally different vision on how the food should be split up. "Drive one truck to the battalion officer's mess and the other to the enlisted men's mess," he ordered.

We blinked at this. There were a couple dozen battalion officers, but over 300 enlisted men left in the Second Battalion. It was far from an even split. However, there was nothing we could do except comply. One truckload of food went to the officers, one to the enlisted men.

It was good to get something solid in our bellies; but in a

few days it was gone and we were back to Jap rice. When the officer's supply began getting low, Captain Finn called me back in. "Do you think you could make another run to the Army dock?" he asked.

"Not twice in a row, sir. I think they will be looking for us now. But give me a couple of trucks and we'll go take a look."

"Same deal," Finn said. "If you get caught, I don't even know you."

Jim Lowe and I rounded up another crew of dependable raiders, loaded onto the two trucks and headed for the hills above Tinian Town. With binoculars, we studied the dock for some time. Not only was there tighter scrutiny of trucks going in and out, but there were armed guards all over the place. This was probably due more to pilfering by the civilian population than anything involving the military, but our chances of a successful foray looked very dim. It was one thing to be living on Jap rice, quite another to be living on bread and water in an Army brig.

"I don't think we can make it," Jim Lowe said at length.

"No. Not at the dock. Let's drive up to the Army supply dump for a look."

We drove up the road in an Army truck column, then pulled off at a little rise overlooking the dump. We didn't worry about the Army truck drivers. They were just doing a hot, boring job and paid no attention to whom other trucks belonged. We did worry about Army Military Police, however. It was the job of MP's to prevent any kind of funny business.

The dump was huge, bigger and busier than anything we had imagined. It covered a couple hundred acres and was laid out precise and neat, probably by military engineers. Crates and cartons were stacked in huge squares with lanes wide enough for a truck to pass between the squares. The perimeter was marked by a double-strand barbed wire fence patrolled by armed guards. With our binoculars we could spot the hardware supplies easily, but the food and boxed-up equipment appeared all alike. While there were lots of guards on the outside rim, security appeared lax inside the perimeter. There were a couple of guards at the entrance and a few sentries sitting on stacks of boxes but that seemed like the full extent. Trucks were going in and out in a steady stream and it didn't look like there was a lot of checking going on like down at the dock.

Anyway, we muddied up our bumpers again to obscure the license numbers, peeled off our Marine dungaree jackets and drove to the entrance with two of our men riding shotgun on each truck running board and a couple in each truck bed. The guards simply waved us through and we drove into the dump like we belonged there. Once inside, we headed up into the section with a lot of boxes, pulled behind a couple of huge stacks and stopped. We split up into two-man teams and scattered out, checking box labels for cartons of food. Fifteen minutes later, we assembled back at the trucks.

The good news was, that the part of the dump with canned fruit and vegetables was a short distance away. The bad news was, there were armed guards posted on top of some stacks of food boxes. We hadn't seen all of them from the hill, but they were apparent now. The food was stacked 10 boxes each way and eight boxes high. Every dozen or so stacks had an armed guard on top.

Corporal Lowe had found a particularly valuable stack, consisting of canned corn beef, canned fruit, canned vegetables and fruit juice, but it was one with a sentry on top. The thing was, the sentry was sound asleep in the sun, slumped over with his rifle on his lap, his head on his chest. We eased our trucks up to the next street over and by standing on the hood of our truck, surveyed the situation. Lowe giggled and said he bet we could take most of the stack out from around the sentry and never wake him up. It sounded like a heck of a challenge, so we set about carrying it out.

Very carefully, we lifted box after box from the stack and

moved them silently to our trucks. In about 20 minutes, we had the whole stack moved except for the double column of boxes that remained directly beneath the sleeping guard. We climbed into our trucks, and drove quickly out of the dump, waving to the sentries at the gate who waved back like we were old friends. We breathed a big sigh of relief. We had made it again!

This time, as we came back to the battalion area, we stopped in a patch of woods down the road and unloaded half of our boxes. Then we drove in with the rest. The captain and the battalion exec officer came over to inspect our booty and were disappointed that the trucks weren't full like in our first raid.

"There are guards all over the place, now, sir," I said with some degree of truth. "We got what we could and then left before we got caught."

The exec officer split the load evenly between the officer's mess and the enlisted men's mess. Later, we sent some men down to the woods and brought the other truckload up to the enlisted mess. This time, the split was 25% to the officers, 75% to the enlisted men, a much more equitable division, particularly since none of the officers ran any risk in the raid.

We had another good supper that night with canned corned beef, canned beans and canned corn with canned pears for dessert. After supper, we sat around the mess tent relating the details of our raid to the rest of Headquarters Company. " I've got only one regret," Jim Lowe said. "I would have given a month's pay to been there when that sentry woke up sitting alone on that skinny stack of boxes and wondered what the heck happened to the big pile he had originally climbed up on to guard."

Chapter 25
Souvenir Hounds

Troops have a habit of collecting souvenirs from everywhere they go. Some combat troops gather a lot of battlefield junk and save it to take home, if they get home. For a few, this becomes almost an obsession. For some, battlefield junk, which we dubbed "Jap Crap" could sometimes be converted into cash or used as trading material. For instance, early at Guadalcanal, souvenir hunters would take a load of battlefield junk down to the beach where the Navy was bringing in supplies. A white silk Jap battle flag with a red rising sun in the middle would sell for $50 or would trade even for a fifth of American whiskey. The same rate held true for a Jap officer's samurai sword. Naval supply personnel usually had cash which they couldn't spend anywhere and often had access to whiskey, no questions asked. Jap flags and samurai swords jumped in value 100% at the docks in San Francisco or San Diego, when the fleet came in. A good trader could double his money if his ship didn't get sunk.

Jap rifles, pistols and combat knives were marketable, but

had a scaled down value. There were problems connected with collecting this junk, other than the fact that Japanese troops did not just hand them over. One problem with picking up Nip stuff was the penchant of the enemy to booby trap a sword or pistol so anyone picking it up would be blown to smithereens. Some dedicated souvenir hounds said they always inspected the stuff very carefully for strings or wires before they picked it up, but this was no guarantee the stuff was safe. Japs could rig a gun or sword with an explosive underneath so lifting the object would set it off.

Many of us did not collect souvenirs because we didn't want to be burdened with any extra stuff. We didn't want any superfluous weight or clutter in a situation where we had to move quickly and needed every little edge to stay alive. And just looking for Jap Crap could be an unnecessary distraction. We never knew how many of our people got killed hunting souvenirs, but it happened. Once a Marine's concentration was taken away from the main job, which was to locate and extirpate the enemy, he was fair game as a target.

Every Marine company had somebody who was pointed out as a bloodthirsty killer. We had one named George Colfax who was known as Killer Colfax. His claim to fame in the souvenir department consisted of small bottle of alcohol in which he carried a pair of Jap ears he said he cut off the first one he shot. That was his story and a lot of newcomers believed it. George liked to get the bottle out, explain what it was, flash it around and put it back in his pack. He was careful not to let anyone handle it or get a real good look at it. None of the old timers paid much attention to all this because somebody saw George whack those ears off a dead Jap pig on Saipan. They were Jap ears all right, but not human ones. Still, it made a good story and it's an even bet that a lot of Marines went home with the story of a guy they knew who had a bottle containing Jap ears.

On Saipan we liberated a lot of civilian homes in the cities of Garapan and Charan Kanoa, and also a lot of farm houses. Many of these were abandoned in haste and the possessions of the owners were still there. Some souvenir hounds picked up silk kimonos, ebony jewel boxes, jewelry, money, fine dishes, paintings, about anything they could haul away. Some guys had the idea of "finders, keepers." Some of us didn't. But not everything liberated was clothing, furnishings or military hardware. Jap drinks like beer and saki were in demand. Japs made good beer and most of this we captured in cases, capped at the brewery. Saki, an alcoholic rice wine, was made by the farmers and was corked. It came in large bottles, about half gallon size, and would give the drinker a pretty fair buzz if it wasn't poisoned. We found out early on that Jap troops sometimes put poison in the saki and left the bottles around where some of our more thirsty and less cautious comrades would get into it. Some men went blind and some died from drinking this stuff. The best rule was not to drink any of their stuff found sitting around. The risk was simply too great.

Among the souvenir hounds in our battalion, the most dedicated, oddly enough, was our battalion chaplain, Father Michaels. This legendary Catholic priest was one of the most fearless men we ever knew. In combat, he came out of his foxhole and rushed to the aid of anybody who got hit. No matter how the world was blowing up around us, Fr. Michaels provided last rites to Catholic boys who took a mortal hit. He was also trained to hold all services, not only for Catholics, but also for some of us who were Protestants. He also knew Jewish rites. He was a remarkable man and beloved by all, but his souvenir hunting created a big problem.

We had no issue with his picking up Jap junk when a battle was over, but he had a habit of always tagging onto any patrol going out. We couldn't very well forbid him going because we had no authority over him. But on patrol, we had to keep an eye on him so he didn't get into any more trouble than needed. Once I had him on a patrol where we were checking out a series of Jap dugouts in a position our troops had overrun along a road. Ostensibly, the dugouts were no longer occupied by live enemy, but the Japs never left a sign outside saying so. Two days before this patrol, another squad had been patrolling a similar situation, and a rookie took a notion to explore a Jap dugout on his own. Before anyone could stop him, he slid halfway into the mouth of the dugout at which point a Jap jammed his rifle against the kid's belly and blew a hole through him. There was this muffled bang and the rest of the patrol came running, realizing the rookie was in trouble. He didn't have enough strength to pull himself out of the entrance and because he was blocking it, nobody could hurl a grenade inside. In terrible pain but realizing what happened, he yelled for a grenade. Somebody handed him one, he pulled the pin and simply held it down inside the dugout, taking out the Jap and finishing himself off. It was an awful incident that never should have happened.

When Father Michaels indicated he was going into a dugout we very quickly persuaded him otherwise, explaining the tragedy two days earlier. We pointed out that we had no proof there were any live Japs in that particular dugout, nor any of the others nearby, but we couldn't simply throw grenades into every hole we came upon. If there was an indication a dugout had residents, we would hurl a grenade inside, but in most cases, we just avoided seeking trouble, assumed the dugouts were empty, but not putting any bets down. We told Father Michaels he could pick up anything he saw lying around but to not go climbing down into any supposedly empty dugouts that just might not be empty. Father Michaels made it through Saipan and Tinian and finished up the war unscathed, a tribute to his faith, luck, or maybe a little of both.

I had pretty much forgotten all about this five years after the war, when I had finished two more years of college and had gone to work as outdoor writer at the Joliet (IL) Herald-News. In my travels, covering fishing, hunting, camping and conservation, I accumulated a file of color slides and I made a few extra bucks putting on slide programs around the Chicago area. One night I was presenting my slide show to a Catholic Men's Club and was startled to see Father Michaels in the crowd. He was in his priest's garb, not a Marine uniform, but he could not be mistaken.

Toward the end of the slide show I held a question and answer session. One of the questions concerned my service in the Marine Corps. For several minutes I entertained the crowd with stories about a battalion priest who was the world's worst souvenir hound. I didn't mention any name, but as I related a number of incidents the crowd laughed uproariously. Through this, the priest's attention became more and more concentrated. At the end of the program, he came up and looked me straight in the eyes. "Were you one of my boys?" he asked, softly.

"Not exactly, Father," I said. "But I was in the same battalion and I will never forget you."

We went over to the coffee table, filled a couple of mugs and spent more than an hour swapping yarns about our war days, reminiscing about the characters we knew, the ones who made it through and the ones who were given last rites on the battlefield. I never did get around to asking Farther Michaels what in the world he did with all that Jap junk he collected, but I am sure it wound up in a museum or in a display case at an American Legion hall somewhere. We shared some laughs and a few tears and solemnly promised to get together for lunch some day to talk some more about the war, but we never did.

Among all the souvenir hounds in the Second Division, we never saw one who could compare with that Catholic Priest who hit the beach with us armed only with his faith in God, the gold crosses on the lapels of his dungarees and a prayer book in his breast pocket.

Chapter 26
Going Home

Luttrell and I were taking no chances with our transportation out. We were at the Tinian airfield an hour early. The field was busy with military planes, cargo planes, plenty of traffic. Our plane was supposed to fly us out at nine, but we had been Marines long enough to be skeptical. In a way, our suspicions were well grounded. The night before, some of the remaining Japs had staged another attack and a lot of our people had been banged up. The Jeeps were bringing them down from the aid stations, two or three at a time, and laying them out along the runway on stretchers for the hospital planes. Apparently, the hospital on Saipan and the hospital ships had all they could handle. These guys were flying straight to Hawaii. That was the first stop for Luttrell and me, too.

Every 30 minutes, an empty Army C-54 landed and a load of waiting casualties went aboard. The stretcher cases deserved and received first priority. What were termed "ambulatory," the ones who could walk, went aboard next. Some, like Luttrell and

I, were simply chronic malaria cases, and we got bumped back as each plane filled up. Luttrell and I were supposed to get on the first plane, but the wounded kept coming in and also sick soldiers more critical than we were. We understood that the Army would give its own troops preference over Marines, but by afternoon, this was getting serious.

"We will have to make a move pretty soon or we'll be here all week," I told Luttrell. "Our priority keeps getting pushed back for stretcher cases and freshly sick soldiers. They are coming in faster than the planes can fly them out."

"What can we do?" Luttrell looked skeptical.

"I got an idea," I said. I had noticed that when a plane came in, two orderlies grabbed each stretcher with a casualty and carried him up the ramp into the plane where he was stored on a rack in the back. Then the orderlies returned for another stretcher. Walking patients were assigned seats to the front. "We're gonna be stretcher bearers," I told Luttrell. He caught on right away and grinned.

We walked to the edge of the runway and picked out a bandaged Marine lying on a stretcher. "You want to get out of here right now?" I asked.

"Yeah, you bet," the kid said.

"Swell. When the next plane comes in, we are going to carry you on board. Just keep your mouth shut."

"Roger, Mac," the wounded kid nodded.

A tan colored C-54 taxied up in a cloud of dust and the engines were switched off. As the ramp was lowered from the cargo door, Luttrell and I grabbed the stretcher and stepped forward quickly. There was a nurse in a crisp white uniform standing by the ramp holding a clipboard. As we went by, she made marks on her clipboard.

Inside the hold of the plane, we found a rack and placed the stretcher on it. "Thanks, Mac," the kid mumbled.

"We're not in the air yet," I warned. We found a couple of

seats ahead of the stretcher racks and sat down, Luttrell on the window side, me on the aisle. The plane filled quickly. The racks were jammed with stretchers and the seats were finally all occupied. The nurse with the clipboard came in, counted heads, checked her tally, nodded and left. The ramp was pulled up and the engines roared. The last view we had of Tinian was two angry-looking soldiers standing on the edge of the runway arguing with the nurse. We hoped they caught the next plane.

We were up maybe 5,000 feet and there was a loud bang in the back of the plane, followed by a gust of cold air howling through the fuselage. A corpsman came by, holding onto the stretcher racks, yelling: "Stay in your seats! Don't anybody go to the rear of the plane!. The hatch ripped open and if you get near the doorway, the wind will suck you out!"

We looked behind us and saw blue sky beyond the rear door. This C-54 looked like it had been flying from the beginning of time. It was an airborne wreck. Because of the opening in the back and the air rushing through, the pilot kept the plane low so we didn't freeze to death. Still, it was cold inside. A lot colder than the island we had just left. We shivered and wrapped our arms around our chests to conserve a little warmth.

Some time went by and the corpsman came back, holding onto the stretcher racks as he moved along. "We are heading for Johnston Island" he announced. "We've got trouble with the outboard engine on the starboard side, but the pilot thinks he can make it O.K."

Luttrell and I looked out and experienced a small stab of concern. The propeller on the far right engine was feathered, not turning. We were flying on three motors instead of four and there was nothing but a lot of ocean below us. We didn't want to think about what would happen if everything quit and we had to ditch the C-54.

Hours went by. Night came on. The plane droned along on three engines wile we dozed in our seats. Eventually it began to get light. Then the plane began to slow up and nose downward. Luttrell had his face pressed against the window glass, trying to spot Johnston Island. "I can't see anything," he said. "We're banking the wrong way."

The other right side engine was smoking as we settled in for our approach. The wheels touched down and the brakes groaned. Over Luttrell's shoulder I could see faces of ground crew personnel standing along the runway. First they looked bored, but then the faces began taking on a look of concern. What the heck was wrong?

Suddenly the plane bumped, shook, wobbled and stopped. We looked out and saw nothing but water. We were sitting in the ocean!

The corpsman came back to reassure us: "Nothing to worry about," he said. "We just overran the runway a little bit. They've got a bulldozer to tow us back up on the runway." I looked at Luttrell and he looked at me. This we didn't need.

When we were finally back on solid ground, the ramp came down and we filed off the C-54. We carried all the stretcher cases off, parked them in the shade and then went looking around at Johnston Island. It didn't seem like much. It was a tiny strip of sand and coral in the middle of the Pacific, between the Marianas and Hawaii. It boasted a runway and a few metal Quonset huts. There were also a couple of small trees which appeared to be recently planted, but well-tended by the base personnel. The heat was blistering.

A soldier in coveralls came over and said there was a Post Exchange in one of the Quonset huts where they had milkshakes. We checked our stretcher case, asked him if we could bring him something and then headed for the PX. Out on the runway we noted lines of "gooney birds," a type of gull that waddled around on the island and had a bad habit of parading in front of moving planes. A lot of gooney birds had become casualties.

The PX was spare but clean and did have excellent chocolate milkshakes. We slurped these and looked out the windows at the white sand, blue ocean, packed runway and legions of gooney birds. When we hit the bottoms of our shakes, we got up, picked up a few treats requested by our stretcher patient and headed back. Mechanics had the cowls off the two huge right hand engines on our C-54.

"Geez, I hope we don't get stuck on this sand pile," Luttrell observed.

"Well, nobody is shooting at us, anyway," I argued.

Crewmen in coveralls were standing on ladders that rested against the motor mounts, working on the engines. Some time went by, then the cowls went back on and the mechanics climbed down. One of the pilots got up on the ramp and yelled for order: "O.K.! We think we've got the trouble fixed and we're going to take off for Hawaii. Anybody who doesn't want to go on this plane can wait for the next one."

There were no takers. We all got back on the C-54, stretcher cases included. We figured we could be sitting here until the end of the war waiting for another plane. All four engines coughed and roared. So far, so good. Our takeoff was smooth and we were out over the blue Pacific, heading for Hawaii. Also, they had fixed the rear door and it was shut tight instead of banging around. We settled back for a quiet ride. "Oh, for cripes sakes!" Luttrell sputtered, pointing out the window. "That outside engine quit again. "

I looked out to see the prop feathered once more. We were back on three engines. But we were aware that a C-54 could fly fine on three. We hoped no more quit.

Somebody behind us said: "The whole Jap army couldn't kill me in the last three years...I hope I don't die in our of our own planes."

It was a thought we all had.

Hours went by as we droned over the water. Afternoon faded into sunset off our stern. The dying sun cast an orange glow on the aluminum wings. Darkness came sudden and total. All we could see was our wing lights blinking in the night. Sometime near midnight an excited voice yelled: "Hawaii ahead!"

From the windows we could see lights. Lights in buildings. Lights on streets. Lights from moving traffic. Then we were between the runway lights, touching down. At that point, the oil line on the other right engine blew. Oil sprayed all over the right side of the plane, blotted out our view from the windows as we went skidding down the runway, the pilots fighting for control. Eventually the crippled bird shuddered to a stop, the ramp came down and we all scrambled off. Ambulances were parked alongside the plane ready for the stretcher cases. Our sense of relief at being on solid ground was overwhelming.

It was sometime before 1 a.m. when the trucks dropped us off at the Aiea Heights Naval Hospital. The lights were on, nurses in crisp white uniforms helped us inside, gave us each pajamas, a towel and a robe and showed us where the hot showers were. Steaming hot water beat down on our bare backs, washing three years of war out of our bodies.

We came out feeling a lot better, ready for bed, but the nurses weren't through with us.

"Anybody like something to eat?'

It had been a long a time since Johnston Island. "What's for chow?" somebody asked.

"Come and see."

We filed into the gleaming hospital dining hall and were astonished to find a menu which provided just about anything we wanted, from steaks to strawberry sundaes! I had fried chicken with mashed potatoes and gravy, topped off with apple pie ala mode. And about six glasses of ice cold milk. Next we filed into a spacious ward. The beds had clean, white sheets and even though dead tired, it took a few minutes to get to sleep. Eventually we collapsed. And slept and slept. It was about 9 a.m. when Luttrell and I woke up and headed for the dining room. Breakfast was scrambled eggs, sausage, toast, grape jam and coffee or milk. No limit on seconds. None of us talked much. We just sort of looked around, took in the spotless surroundings and savored the food.

Before noon, we had fresh underwear and socks, clean khaki uniforms and began to look presentable. And as we regained our strength, we also regained the other traits of young warriors loaded with testosterone. Everybody asked the nurses their names, where they were from and what they were doing after they got off duty. They sure looked good to us, but they had seen a lot of raunchy Marines, and although cheerful and friendly, they kept us at arm's length. Well, more like a cot's length.

Over the next couple of days, we saw every base movie, played basketball in the gym and read every magazine in the place. Then orders came through directing us to board a hospital ship for the states. We told all the nurses goodbye, professed our undying love, said we would come back after the war and marry them all. They said they would wait for us, even the ones who were married. They were good at this. We were probably the umpteenth bunch of Marines to pass through since Pearl Harbor.

Then we rode buses to a big, white hospital ship, climbed aboard, watched fascinated as tugs pulled us away from the dock and we got underway for the mainland. The voyage now is hazy and I can only recall drinking a lot of coffee late at night, smoking cigarettes and telling endless war stories. Word came down one morning with the electrifying news that we were coming into San Francisco.

We carried all the stretcher cases up to the main deck and placed them facing forward. There were other Marines lining the rail, up on the superstructure, anywhere there was a foothold, as we cruised underneath the Golden Gate and into San Francisco Harbor. As we warped up to the dock, a band was playing a Sousa march. We were pretty well choked up. There as not a dry eye in the crowd. Not even the guys on the stretch-ers.

Home! The word kept hammering in our heads. Home! Migod, we made it home!

* * * * * * * *

From San Francisco we boarded a train that took us to the Naval Hospital at Bainbridge, Maryland. Some of us who lived in the Midwest had put in for the Naval Hospital at Great Lakes, but the train took us right through Chicago to the east coast. Indeed, we paused in Chicago for about 40 minutes and found all the doors in the train locked so we couldn't get off. The military was taking no chances on somebody turning up missing in Chicago. The most noteworthy happening on our cross-country safari was our arrival in Bainbridge at 2 a.m. We were ushered down a winding corridor and into a large, dimly lit ward where a nurse and a couple of corpsmen in white dungarees assigned us to our bunks. We had just gotten settled when the phone rang in the ward and the nurse came down the rows of cots asking for volunteers to go to the front office and bring in some stretcher cases. We were tired, but still dressed, so about 15 of us filed down the vacant hall to the glassed-in office. We could see no stretchers or patients. Behind the glass was a beefy Master at Arms in Navy whites sitting in the office grinning at us. First Sergeant Mahoney went to the window and yelled: "Where are the stretcher cases?'

The Master at Arms laughed out loud and said there weren't any. "I thought it was time for you Marines to get up and go to the toilet so you didn't wet the bed," he roared, obviously very impressed with his own humor.

The First Sergeant let out a bellow of rage, his fist shat-tered the glass window of the office and he went over the counter and into the office, trailed by a half dozen highly incensed Ma-rines. I had one glimpse of a terror-stricken Master at Arms back-ing away from the invasion and then I lit out for the ward. I

240

didn't know what was going to happen but whatever it was, I didn't want to be any part of it.

About 20 minutes later, the First Sergeant and his assault troops walked back into the ward, laughing. "What happened?" somebody inquired. Seems that the First Sergeant charged into the Master at Arms, decked him with a right haymaker, dragged him over to the duty desk and rang up the base commander, a full Navy Captain, getting him out of bed. "This is First Sergeant Mahoney, United States Marine Corps!" Mahoney announced. "I am sitting on the chest of a Master At Arms by the name of..." and he read off the man's name and serial number. "You better send somebody down to retrieve him."

In minutes, the Navy Captain, in person, and a half dozen shore police arrived ready for combat. Interestingly enough, when they looked at the broken window and got the story from the First Sergeant, the Captain placed the errant Master at Arms under arrest and sent the Marines back to the ward.

It was that easy. The Navy Captain knew who we were and where we had come from and he didn't take any pleasure in a Navy desk jockey giving combat Marines a bad time. We had no further run-ins with base personnel at Bainbridge. On the other hand, we did enjoy our first shore leave in the United States. It was a short train ride from the hospital to the Baltimore seafood emporiums where a half dozen oysters and a tall glass of beer cost one dollar. Well, not even that. Three of us from the Second Divison sort of hung around together - P.F.C. Chick Owens from Chilton, Wisconsin, a corporal I remember only by his nickname "Memphis" and I. We all had fat rolls of Japanese money from the bank in Saipan and we would order three beers, then toss some 10,000 yen bills on the bar.

"What the heck is that stuff?" the bartender would ask.

"Jap money," we told him.

"Is it any good?"

"It is in Japan."

This usually was good for a laugh from the bartender and any customers at the bar. Apparently, we were the first combat Marines back from the war to hit this part of Baltimore and they treated us very well. We not only paid for our beer with Jap 10,000 yen notes, but the bartenders usually pinned a bill or two on the wall behind the bar for souvenirs. Some of that Jap money may still be pinned up behind those bars.

Chapter 27
Winding Down

It was just a few days before Christmas, 1944, when we boarded a train for Great Lakes Naval Station near Chicago. The three of us who lived in the Midwest, Owens, "Memphis," and myself, had been trying for weeks to get to the Great Lakes Naval Hospital ever since we landed at Bainbridge, Maryland. Owens was 18 years old. He had nearly three years overseas. You can figure how old he was when he enlisted. Three days before Christmas, we arrived at Great Lakes, busting to go home. Before checking in at the hospital, we took the precaution of stopping at the Marine Guard Company barracks to talk with the laundry truck driver. Why the truck driver? Because we knew from experience that there was quite often a hang-up when one sought the necessary documents to get out of a base. We received assurance from the driver of the laundry truck that if we got stalled with paperwork, we could slip out of the naval base in the back of his truck, covered with laundry bags. After all, it was Christmas time.

With that detail taken care of, we proceeded to check in at the hospital. We were assigned to a large ward containing about 70 or more congenial sailors-in-training with various complaints from ankle sprains to back pains. A friendly nurse and a businesslike corpsman ushered us to three adjoining bunks. It was apparent we were the first combat Marines to grace the ward.

"Is there anything more we can do for you?" the nurse asked.

"Yes ma'am," said Chick. "You can get us leave papers so we can go home for Christmas."

"I don't think so."

"Why not?"

"All Christmas leave requests had to be in two weeks ago. It's too late for that."

"We weren't here two weeks ago."

"Yes. Well that's too bad. Maybe sometime after New Year's."

We kept sorting out our gear, putting some in the small chests of drawers alongside our bunks, the balance in our duffle bags. The nurse kept watching us intently. "What are you putting in the duffle bags?" she asked.

"Stuff we need to go home for Christmas."

"Wait a minute," she said, looking worried. "I'll have to get the doctor." She went rushing down the ward, her heels clicking on the hardwood floor. In one minute she was back with the doctor, a young Lieutenant Commander.

"What are you doing?" the doctor asked.

"Packing to go home for Christmas, sir," Memphis replied, smiling.

"All the leaves had to be applied for two weeks ago. You can't go right now."

"Yes, sir," Memphis said as we kept packing our clothes and toilet articles.

"Look!" the doctor said with obvious frustration. "You

244

Marines could get in a lot of trouble!"

With that statement we simply fell apart. Chick Owens sagged against his cot, laughing. Memphis doubled over and. I laughed so hard tears ran down my face..

"Trouble? We...could...get...in...trouble?" Chick gasped. "Oh, migod, Doc! You don't know what the hell trouble is."

The doctor's neck turned a trifle red and he glared at us. He no doubt sensed that he had three uncooperative Marines on his hands who were well acquainted with trouble. On the other hand, the last thing he needed as a Christmas present was to file a report to higher authority that three patients were somehow missing from his ward.

"Don't go anywhere!" he ordered. "I'll be right back!" He took off for the door at a fast clip. We calmly finished our packing, then locked our duffle bags shut. At that point, the doctor came rushing back waving some papers. He gave us each furlough papers granting 30-day emergency leaves. How he did it, we never knew; but he must have pushed the right buttons somewhere. After three years we were going home! We solemnly thanked the doctor and the nurse, saluted and left them staring as we headed for the door. It was a nice feeling to walk out the front gate of the base legally instead of sneaking out under a pile of laundry.

I never saw Owens or Memphis again. I don't know if they went back overseas, even if they are still living. But I have a vivid memory of that day at the Great Lakes Naval Hospital when the doctor warned us we might "get in trouble." Hoo, boy!

It was evening and snowing when I swung off the train at the station in my hometown of Joliet, Illinois. The store windows were all brightly decorated for Christmas with red, blue, green and yellow lights that reflected off the swirling snowflakes. Recorded Christmas music echoed softly up the streets punctuated by the steady ringing of bells wielded by Salvation Army volunteers leaning over their iron kettles. Crowds of shoppers hustled along the sidewalk, laughing, exchanging greetings. The marquee on the front of the Princess Theater listed a western movie in bright lights. I tossed my sea bag in the backdoor of a taxi and headed for home.

Christmas was a gala affair at home with my mom, dad and sister. Relatives came from everywhere and I got a little tired answering questions about the war. I knew what they wanted to hear - some kind of heroics - not the mud and blood and stench and insects and dysentery. Like most returnees, I got edgy and wandered downtown to swap stories with other men home on leave. The gathering point for most servicemen was the Louis Joliet Lounge, known as the "Looie." Everybody came there - Army, Navy, Air Force and Marines - all during the war. Indeed it was at the Looie some months later that I finally caught up with my old hometown Marine buddy from Saipan, Hamilton Lyons. I was sitting at a table one evening talking war with Glen Goodson, a returned Army pilot who flew observation for General Stillwell in Burma. An uproar erupted up at the bar and I moseyed over to see what all the noise was all about. There were maybe 15 soldiers and sailors an civilians in a half circle around somebody who was yelling up a storm.

"It's Ham Lyons," somebody explained. "He came home from the Marine Corps with battle fatigue and is threatening to kill somebody!"

I hadn't seen Lyons since we sat out the Jap air raid together in the hospital tent on Siapan, but I knew he was not any nuttier than the rest of us. I elbowed my way through the throng and came face-to-face with Lyons who had obviously been imbibing for some time and was putting on quite a show. He was waving a beer bottle around, threatening to knock the head off anybody who got within reach.

"Hey, Lyons!" I yelled at him. His eyes came somewhat back in focus. "Listen, Hammy, you can blow smoke up these recruits but don't try to pull that battle fatigue crap on this old

Marine! Put the bottle down!"

Lyons took a good look, recognized me, laughed and dropped the bottle on the bar. "Hey, let's have a drink," he suggested.

I invited him over to our table and he sat down with Goodson and me. Over a cold one, I told Goodson about Lyons' short term combat record - getting hit the first day on Tarawa and repeating the performance on D-day on Saipan.

"That's not all, "Lyons laughed. "I got nailed again at Okinawa."

"The heck?"

"Yeah. Didn't even make it to the beach. A Kamikaze blew our troop ship in half. A Navy boat fished me out of the water. Got my shoulder smashed, but the doctors fixed it up so I could get home for Christmas. So now I've got three invasions, hit three times, three purple hearts and only seven hours in combat."

We all laughed so hard we had tears in our eyes. I ordered another round.

After 30 days of visiting, meeting relatives and friends of friends, I was ready to go back. There was a lot of war still going on, but it seemed to be winding down, at least on paper. Germany was finished. Japan strictly on defense. After Christmas leave, our group of returned Marines was assigned several weeks of guard duty at Great Lakes. One assignment was to herd 150 prisoners from the stockade across the street to a mess hall, watch them being fed, then run them back to the lockup. As Sergeant of the Guard on the detail outside the stockade, my job was to stand behind the gate with a loaded Colt .45, unlock the gate, step back and watch the 150 prisoners dash across the street between two barricades manned by four Marines with sawed-off shotguns.

These were all Navy and Marine prisoners awaiting trial for everything from robbery to assault, perhaps murder. They were a tough bunch and we took no chances with any of them. One noon, just as I was set to unlock the gate, two young Navy Lt. Commanders came out of the officer's mess just up the street and attempted to take a short cut through the barricaded corridor, even though signs declared this area off limits to anyone except guards and prisoners. I heard one of the guards challenge the officers and then explain briefly that we were running prisoners to the mess hall and no one was allowed to trespass. One of the officers laughed, waved a hand at the guard, said O.K., they were just crossing to the next street and they would go around the other way after that.

The guard, holding them back with his sawed-off shotgun, looked up at me and yelled: "Hey, what a should I do, Sarge?"

"If they try to cross the line, shoot 'em," I said, tersely. With that, I swung the gate back and let the prisoners go running for the mess hall. The officers jumped back as the mass of prisoners thundered through the off-limits area. They could have been in the middle of 150 somewhat unsavory characters.

When the prisoners vanished into the mess hall, one of the officers, red with anger, came over and copied my name off my badge. He subsequently went to the guard company HQ and filed a complaint. When I came off duty I was called into headquarters where a very grim captain sat drumming on his desk with a pencil. "Dammit, Cary, I have a report that you ordered a guard to shoot a couple of Navy officers," the Captain growled.

"No, sir," I replied. "Those officers were trying to crash through the 'Off Limits' area where we run the prisoners, and it is well-marked with signs. When the guard challenged them, they tried to laugh it off and bluff their way through. The guard asked me what to do. I said if they tried it, to shoot them. It was just something to scare them."

The captain cupped his chin with both hands. "Omigod," he said. "Listen, this is a Navy Base and we've got to get along with these people."

"They were wrong, sir," I reiterated. "They were trying to pull rank to get past the guard. I couldn't let that happen."

"They must have been steaming," the Captain said.

"Not at first, sir. At first they turned white and looked scared."

"Oh, boy!" the Captain sucked in his breath. "You guys back from combat think you are tough as hell."

"We are tough as hell, Captain."

At that, he grinned a little. "Yeah....well, try to get along with them the best you can and for cripe's sake don't threaten to shoot them!"

"Yes sir!" Luckily, that was the end of it.

From Great Lakes we were sent to duty at Camp Pendleton, San Diego, where we were assigned to combat replacement units. By spring, Germany was ready to surrender, but Japan kept on fighting. We knew they would fight to the last soldier and last civilian. It was their way.

It had been on April 1, that the Second Division had hit the beach at Okinawa with the First and Sixth Marine Divisions, along with the 24th Army Corps. It was a great April Fool's Day surprise for the Empire of the Rising Sun. There were an estimated 100,000 heavily-armed elite Japanese troops stationed there, the best Japan had to offer. Losing Okinawa, the Japanese knew, opened the door for an invasion of the mainland. They went all out to keep that from happening.

The Japanese also threw most of their remaining air and naval forces against the Okinawa invasion. In the ensuing sea and air battle, both the U.S. carriers Enterprise and Hancock were hit and disabled, but what was left of the Jap fleet was sent reeling into retreat. Their air force was in tatters; but they had no thought of surrender. Daily, we read accounts of the grinding land battle. Daily, troop planes flew out of California with Marine reinforcements headed for combat. It didn't make any difference what our specialty was. We were all riflemen, all returned combat veterans, all slated to be fitted in wherever needed.

As the battle got hotter, casualties escalated and replacement flights were speeded up. An order came through cleaning out all base personnel who had been on duty at Camp Pendleton since the beginning of the war. They were shipped straight to Okinawa and some of us were used as temporary fill-ins. A notice was posted that a sign painter was needed to replace the one heading overseas. Having done a little sign work prior to the war, I applied and was sent over to the base sign shop, a little hole in the wall adjacent to the carpenter shop.

Inside the sign shop, a curly-haired young Marine was painting a name on an officer's locker box. He looked at me and lay his brush down. "Are you the guy"?' he asked.

"I'm the guy."

The Marine stuck out his hand. "Corporal Danny Dedo," he said. "You'll find everything you need here. The brushes are all clean and in order...paints are in the cabinets. Give me an hour and then come back?"

I said "sure" and wandered outside. An hour later I came back. Dedo was gone. On the door he had hung a sign with a gold star, like the ones gold star mothers who gave their sons to the war hung in windows all across the United States.

Under the gold star, a sign read: "Danny Dedo Went to War."

Reports indicated the killing on Okinawa was intense. It wasn't just grunts in the foxholes. Army General Simon Bolivar Buckner was killed. So was famed war correspondent Ernie Pyle. Daily, the planes left San Diego jammed with Marines. It was now just a matter of time until we all went. And after Okinawa we knew the next stop would be the beaches of Japan itself. Estimates were that from 250,000 to a half million American troops would die invading the Japanese Mainland. Estimated Japanese casualties were figured at several million.

Those of us still in California were aware that we were the guys with the experience, skilled in the mechanics of war. And, we knew Marines would lead the charge. Our odds, not good to start with, would shrink fast. We didn't relish the idea, but we were prepared to deal with it. War was our business.

Daily bombing raids by B-29's were tearing into the Japanese mainland defenses, but it would still take an enormous landing force to conquer the mainland. By June, Okinawa was winding down but already 50,000 Americans had been killed or wounded there. Some 110,000 Japanese had been killed and over 7,000 captured. The time was fast approaching for the final mainland invasion. Allied forces had demanded that Japan surrender, but without success. None of us knew that two atomic bombs were being readied for delivery from that same Tinian airfield the Second and Fourth Divisions had taken in early summer.

August 6, the first nuclear weapon was detonated over Hiroshima. Two days later, Nagasaki was hit. The entire world was stunned by the devastation. The attitude was slightly different in the barracks at Camp Pendleton. There was a feeling of relief, that there would be no invasion, that Japan was finally finished. August 10, the Japanese offered to surrender. The word we got was that the emperor had called in the hard core military high command and told them the war was over. The Japanese military, quite ready to die to the man and take the entire country with them, bowed to the Emperor's wishes. On August 14, the Emperor accepted all allied demands. The war finally ended. U.S. forces were sent to occupy Japan. It looked like some of us would soon be out of a job.

At Camp Pendleton, the daily routine changed. No more planeloads of replacements flying out. No more task forces were needed, no more landings, no more beachheads, no more killing and dying. It was hard to believe, but it was over. All that remained now was to get discharged and go home.

To process troops for discharge, the Marine Corps had devised a point system. A fixed number of points were given for each combat invasion, so many points for total time overseas, so many points for each medal, each purple heart, for total time in the Pacific. Three of us in our barracks, all original Guadalcanal veterans, had the highest number of points. All three of us were summoned to headquarters to sign our discharge papers. By alphabetical order, I was the first one in the door. I saluted a sharp-faced Second Lieutenant sitting at a desk, smiling like a hungry piranha. It seemed like there was always a sharp-faced second lieutenant that looked like a piranha behind every desk in every headquarters we ever walked into. He pushed some papers toward me. "The nation is grateful for your splendid service," the piranha said. "We want to get you home in a hurry. Sign right here."

My eyebrows went up. How did he know if the nation was grateful or if I had a splendid service record? From long experience, I looked at what I was signing. The words "U.S. Marine Corps Reserve" jumped out at me. "No, sir," I said, firmly. "No reserve status. I want out, completely."

The Lieutenant looked very disappointed. "We can process you right now if you sign up for the reserves," he said, frowning. "If you want full discharge, it may take some time longer."

Heck of a game. I thanked the piranha, saluted and strode out the door. "Look out!" I told the next two men. "They're running a reserve sign-up scam." It looked like the lieutenant was getting brownie points for everyone he persuaded to sign up for the reserves.

One at a time, the other two high-point Marines went in, saluted, looked at the papers and filed out without signing. Reserves we did not want to be. We wanted out. Some of the men who filed in behind us did sign up for the reserves and went directly home. And a number of them were called up for service a few years later in Korea.

The majority of us, however, at least the old timers, opted for a clear discharge. If there was another war, we wanted the freedom of choice. And so we went back to the barracks to wait.

We didn't even go to San Diego for a movie because we wanted to be right there in case our names came up. We played a lot of cards, poker being the most popular game. And we complained a lot.

We thought it was a lousy way to treat combat troops. On the other hand, nobody was shooting at us. No foxholes to dig. No K-rations. Under those circumstances, we could sit for quite awhile.

We were playing the usual nickel-dime poker one day when PFC Clayton Fiske walked over and said he was going to call his father. "My dad is a close friend of our Senator and a lot of big people in Washington. He'll see to it that we get discharged and sent home right away"

We all cracked up laughing. Fiske was pretty much pegged as a blowhard. He was always telling us how important his father was and who he knew. "Sure," somebody said. "You just call your daddy, Fiske, and he'll get us all sent home right away."

"Well, I will. Only I need some quarters for the pay phone Can you guys chip in some quarters?"

This created another round of hilarity. Sure. Fisk was going to call his very important father who knows U.S. Senators and he needed to borrow quarters from us to do it. Still laughing, we pulled a fistful of quarters out of the poker pot and handed them to Fisk who vanished in the direction of a pay phone.

A little later he returned and announced: "Well, I talked with my dad and he is going to get the Senator in on this and it will be all straightened out." That created more laughter. We went back to our poker game determined to outwait and outwit the base command.

Behold and lo! The next morning, just before noon, an Army C-54 landed on the Camp Pendleton runway and off strode a U.S. Senator and his staff, followed by a general and assorted military brass. We didn't get to hear what the Senator or the general said to the Camp Pendleton commander, but it must have

253

been something persuasive. Immediately after lunch, all of us on the "No Reserve" list were hustled through the base facilities - laundry, library, PX, quartermaster and paymaster - to determine if we owed any money anywhere, and lastly to the piranha wearing second lieutenant bars, who was no longer smiling and who had us sign our papers. Then we were summarily trucked to the San Diego railroad station, tickets and discharges in hand, and waved goodbye to the Marine Corps.

The war, after nearly four years, was finally over. The wounded, in naval and military hospitals, had a lot of repair work before they could go home. Some, like the permanently disabled, wound up in Veterans Administration facilities, and would never make it home. For many of them the war would never end.

Those of us who returned to civilian life found that the veterans of World War I, survivors of the blood-spattered trenches in France in 1917-1918, had successfully lobbied legislation through the Congress providing us with many benefits they never had such as a G. I. Bill of Rights guaranteeing college education to those of us who wanted it. We can never adequately express our gratitude.

Taps

At the end of the day, at sunset, when the colors are being taken down, the bugle sounds taps. It is now taps for those of us who fought in the Pacific.

Time moves on. World War II was 60 years ago. The survivors are rapidly dying off. Our numbers dwindle every month. Gray-haired, bald-headed, wrinkled and aging, we assemble every Memorial Day at the nation's cemeteries to salute the colors, to recite the Pledge of Allegiance and to pay our respects to those no longer with us.

Every Nov. 10, many of we old Marines gather, those of us who are still able, at VFW and Legion halls across the nation. We gather to honor the birthday of the United States Marine Corps, Nov. 10, 1775. It is a long and proud history of men who served in every war involving our nation plus those women who served from World War II to the present. We have a saying: "Once a Marine, always a Marine."

Each of us, if our nation was attacked and if we were able, would not hesitate to go again. We know war. We know its horrors, its ear-shattering din, and its pain and stench. We are members of the warrior clan, something little known and less understood by the public at large. Our loyalties are fierce: first to our nation and its flag and second to our comrades in the Marine Corps.

It is what we are, who we are. And we make no apology. For whatever transgressions we may have committed in the eyes of the world, we have made our peace with God.

O.K., bugler. Now you may sound taps.

About the Author

Ex-Marine Sergeant Bob Cary served with the Second Division, USMC, in World War II from 1942 to 1945 when the war finally ended. He was in combat with the Division at Guadalcanal, Tarawa, Saipan and Tinian. The Division ended its service to the nation at Okinawa. At the war's end, Cary was at Camp Pendleton, California, training for the invasion of Japan which did not become necessary when Japan surrendered on September 2, 1945 after an attempt was made by hard core Japanese military personnel to prevent the Emperor from accepting the terms of surrender.

The Second Marine Division suffered 12,395 combat casualties in the war. Coupled with malaria and other diseases, plus accidents and training losses, the division had over 100% replacement of personnel. President Franklin Roosevelt awarded the division the Presidential Unit Citation for storming the atoll of Tarawa, Nov. 20, 1943, in which 3,100 Marines went down in three days.

During the war, eight division members received the Congressional Medal of Honor, most posthumously. Medal of Honor recipient David M. Shoup later became Commandant of the Marine Corps.

Following service in the Marines, Bob Cary became a reporter with the Joliet Herald News and the Chicago Daily News. He was married to Lillian (Kluge) and was father of two daughters, Marjorie and Barbara. He moved to Ely, Minnesota in 1966 and opened a wilderness canoe trip and guiding service. In 1974 he became editor of the Ely Echo newspaper and is still employed there as a columnist. He has had nine books published and countless magazine articles. His wife Lillian died in 1993. He remarried a widowed family friend, Edith Sommer, and they now live in the Superior National Forest northeast of Ely near the Canadian border.

"There are very few of us left now from the old Second Division," Cary notes. "It is well that our record in World War II be recalled at a time when the survival of the nation is at stake. It is well to know what kind of people the Marine Corps, the Army, Navy, Air Force and Coast Guard require to do the job."

The author is no advocate for war. "No one hates war more than those who have been there, who know first hand its chaos, noise, pain, stench and horror," he notes. "But when our nation is threatened, citizens always rise up in defense, from Lexington and Concord to this day. We have always volunteered to lay our lives on the line for our families, friends, neighbors and fellow citizens.

"In addition to being highly trained and highly-motivated Marines, we were also young, wild, irrepressible and full of wry humor even into battle. We took our mission seriously, but not ourselves. We fully recognized our mortality and the odds we faced.

"That is who we were. That is who we are to this day. And we make no apologies to anyone."